EXPERIMENT WITH FREEDOM

CHATHAM HOUSE ESSAYS

Previous essays in the series have been:

The Royal Institute of International Affairs is an unofficial body which promotes the scientific study of international questions and does not express opinions of its own. The opinions expressed in this publication are the responsibility of the author.

The Institute gratefully acknowledges the comments and suggestions of the following who read the manuscript on behalf of the Research Committee: E. W. R. Lumby, Professor P. N. S. Mansergh, and Sir Archibald Nye.

Experiment with Freedom

INDIA AND PAKISTAN, 1947

BY
HUGH TINKER

Issued under the auspices of the
Royal Institute of International Affairs

OXFORD UNIVERSITY PRESS

LONDON   BOMBAY   KARACHI

1967

*Oxford University Press, Ely House, London W.*1

GLASGOW NEW YORK TORONTO MELBOURNE WELLINGTON
BOMBAY CALCUTTA MADRAS KARACHI LAHORE DACCA
CAPE TOWN SALISBURY NAIROBI IBADAN
KUALA LUMPUR HONG KONG TOKYO

*Printed in Great Britain
by The Eastern Press Ltd.
of London and Reading*

To DAVID

For whom it is history

And some are sung, and that was yesterday
And some **unsung,** *and that may be tomorrow*

An Acknowledgement

A NUMBER of people have helped in the preparation of this book although, of course, the interpretation of the events described is my own. It was my good fortune that the text was read by E. W. R. Lumby, Nicholas Mansergh, and Sir Archibald Nye. Their careful vigilance has helped to give more precision to the narrative. Among colleagues, I have discussed most aspects of the transfer of power at great length, especially with S. R. Mehrotra, C. H. Philips, and Z. H. Zaidi.

This is the second of my books which Valerie Lowenhoff has typed with marvellous accuracy, while Hermia Oliver has for the third time exercised her unique editorial skill on my work, deftly combining restraint, sensibility, and authority. Once again, Elisabeth, my wife, has been both my most kind and most severe critic. This book was written at high pressure, and this entailed a good deal of forbearance by her, and by my sons, throughout a long vacation.

November 1966   H.T.

Contents

9. Consequences and Causes—*cont.*

I

Introduction

BETWEEN August 1947 and May 1948, five new independent nation-states came into being in lands where Britain had ruled. Although subsequent years were to see a cavalcade of new nations emerge from the old British Empire, nothing quite like this first experiment in freedom was ever again experienced. Between them, these five cases represented almost every variety of decolonization. The first two nations to emerge—the subject of this essay—provided the greatest test. The Indian National Congress, one of the oldest political organizations of the modern world, had campaigned for self-government for forty years, and for twenty-five years had challenged the British to transfer power without delay and on their terms. For most of this time, the Congress had stood forth as the only real political party in India: yet at a late hour a rival had appeared, the reborn Muslim League, and had in turn challenged the right of the Congress to speak for all India. Faced with two rival movements, both appealing to deep feelings within the Indian sub-continent, the British attempted to bring the parties together: then, failing to secure agreement on co-operation, at the last moment succeeded in securing agreement to divide, and coexist as two nations. The two nations entered independence as willing members of the British Commonwealth. Perhaps this development was, ultimately, of less significance than at the time appeared: but without doubt the new concept of Commonwealth membership which this set in motion was an asset of immense value in smoothing the process of British decolonization.

Out of conflict came agreement: this was an achievement which stabilized the uncertain, uncharted voyage from empire to independence. It might so easily have been different, as the other cases of the day were to show.

Alternative routes to independence

When Burma attained independence in January 1948, this resulted from the defiance of Britain by the young nationalist group, the Anti-Fascist People's Freedom League, and their daemonic leader, Aung San. The first British statement of policy on Burma, issued in May 1945, would have postponed even a return to the self-government enjoyed before 1942 until December 1948. Aung San rallied the masses by an inflammatory campaign; staged nation-wide strikes, and brought the public services to a standstill. By these methods he induced the Governor to discard all the other political contenders for power and to recognize Aung San as virtual Prime Minister. Having ruthlessly stamped upon the attempts of the communists to turn his own methods of physical force against his new government, Aung San came to London to confront the Prime Minister. On 27 January 1947 he secured an undertaking which he summarized as 'full independence within one year'. Returning to Burma, he negotiated an agreement with the minority peoples who now threw in their lot with the AFPFL: except for the Karens, the largest of these indigenous minorities, who could not be won over. A Committee of Inquiry sent out by the British government was unable to reconcile the Karens with the Burmese. Nevertheless, a Constituent Assembly was convened, and between June and September produced a constitution, whereby Burma became a republic: outside the British

Commonwealth. In July Aung San was assassinated: everything might have been put back, but U Nu came forward as Prime Minister, and in October went to London to sign a treaty with Britain, whereby Burma became 'a fully independent sovereign state'.

In Burma a determined leader was able to set aside the British timetable, crush his rivals, and ignore a recalcitrant minority. The nation's destiny was formally decided by a Constituent Assembly, popularly elected, but totally committed to Aung San and the AFPFL. The sole function of the British government was to register its acceptance of these actions by treaty. Independence was a triumph of will for Aung San. Yet by carrying through an independence which did not satisfy the hopes and fears of the Karen minority, the country was fated to suffer civil war which, almost twenty years later, shows no sign of ending. Beside the Karens, other dissatisfied minorities, Shans, Kachins, and Mons, have joined the revolt. Perhaps because the constitution was hurried through, it was devised in accord with theoretical ideology, rather than to meet the needs of the peoples of Burma. Fifteen years later, the constitution was torn up by the military leaders who forcibly seized power. At the time of writing it has not been replaced.

The next experiment in independence could hardly have afforded a greater contrast to the Burmese experience. When, in February 1948, the Duke of Gloucester formally conveyed the congratulations of King George VI to the people of Ceylon on their attainment of independence, an uninformed spectator might have been bewildered to discover exactly what had changed. Following Ceylon's valiant support of the British war-effort, a Commission headed by Lord Soulbury recommended that Ceylon should acquire full internal self-government. Legislation to this effect was prepared, but meanwhile events in India showed that in the sub-continent the outcome of the negotiations would, or could, be complete independence. The Ceylonese ministers who had functioned as a 'Cabinet' and War Council represented to the British government that this discrimination against a loyal colony was inequitable, and their protest was accepted. By additions and modifications, the proposals for internal self-government were amplified to give full independence.

Ceylon already enjoyed universal suffrage, but there were modifications in the electoral system, while the system of government by Boards was replaced by conventional Cabinet government on the Westminster model.

The astute national leader, Don S. Senanayake, who arranged this acceleration of the process of political development, formed a popular political organization— the United National Party—on the threshold of independence. But the attainment of freedom was the work of the few, not of the many. The outward symbols of sovereignty remained much as before. True, the Lion flag replaced the Union Jack, but the Governor-General still continued to dwell in King's House, as the Crown representative in a Dominion, and the defence agreement with Britain permitted the Royal Navy and Royal Air Force to retain staging-posts and bases. When these forces were requested to withdraw in 1956, the agreement fell into desuetude but was not formally abrogated.

Doubtless this painless, almost invisible transition into independence caused little if any dislocation in the life of Ceylon. But independence without tears sowed its own delayed harvest of thorns. The Tamil minority and the Christian community were not disturbed in 1948: but the problem of their assimilation or isolation had to be tackled sooner or later. The first attempt made after 1956 was little short of disastrous, and left scars which ten years later had not entirely healed. Moreover, the attainment of independence without any popular involvement seemed to leave the political parties lacking a sense of identification with the ordinary people. Nowhere does independence create nationhood: but it can, as it were, take the lid off and reveal what nation-building is going to be about. In Ceylon, the test of nationhood seems to have been unduly postponed by the almost effortless and somewhat meaningless independence of February 1948.

The last of this group of new nations, Israel, came into being in May 1948. This event showed British policy in a state of bankruptcy; and total chaos was only averted by the amazing *élan* of the Jewish people. From 1937 Britain had attempted to find a solution in Palestine which would accommodate the ingathering of the Jews and yet satisfy the indigenous Arab population and the Muslim world of the Middle East. First, Britain was compelled to fight an Arab rising. Then, after the second world war, when the uprooted Jews of Eastern Europe attempted to land in Palestine and were turned back, Jewish extremists launched an underground war on British officials and security forces. The future of Palestine was referred to the new United Nations organization, where the problem ran into the growing tensions between East and West. After much delay, a solution was proposed on the basis of the partition of Palestine between Jewish and Arab areas, with a loose overall union. When this plan was accepted by the Jews but rejected by the Arabs, the British government decided to terminate the mandate unilaterally. In mid-May, the last of the British troops were evacuated through Haifa while, all around the harbour, Arabs and Jews were fighting for their lives. Out of battle, the state of Israel came to life: but its emergence owed little to the retiring British. The divided city of Jerusalem, the unslaked hatred of Arabs inside and outside Palestine, Israeli defiance; these were the tragic memorials of the departing British in Israel.

Questions and answers

These extraordinary variations on the theme of decolonization have been recalled as a reminder that British policy
after the second world war was being evolved *ad hoc*. The
Labour government was conscious of the urgent need to
begin that long process of shedding commitments which a
war-impoverished Britain could no longer maintain. But
how were countries long held under British rule to be transformed into independent nations? The precedents were
not helpful. Canada, Australia, and the Union of South
Africa had been assisted into self-government at a relatively simple stage of political development. There, the
problem was not so much that of resolving differences
between the metropolitan country and the colony, or
between conflicting forces in the colony, as it was of
building the fabric of nationhood out of rather primitive
elements. The formula of consolidation: drawing together
separate colonies into a wider entity, had been employed
in all three cases to give some overall strength to the dis-
connected parts. Even when the European cultural in-
heritance was divided, as in Canada and South Africa,
these divisions were masked because after federation and
union political leadership was firmly held by men of
British stock, or by French Canadians or Afrikaners who
were strongly under British cultural influence (somewhat
like the Ceylonese leaders immediately after independence). The grant of self-government by Britain had been
made before either relations with the *métropole* or internal
relations had matured to a point where there was conflict.[1]

The last episode, the emergence of Ireland as an
independent nation, offered grim warnings, but gave little

[1] Of course there had been a conflict in South Africa between British and
Boer cultural concepts, but to all appearances the conflict had been ended
by the acceptance of a British hegemony.

promise of how self-government might be successfully promoted. For over thirty years, a debate had continued in the British parliament as to the ultimate status of Ireland and had shaken internal party relationships more than any other issue of modern times. Having at last moved towards Home Rule, the British government discovered after the first world war that there was no longer any political party with whom they could negotiate: the moderate men had vanished. There followed an attempt to suppress a people under arms by the application of physical force: approaching, at one point, the use of terror. Fortunately, the British government pulled back from this road without an ending, and at the last moment succeeded in negotiating with the adversary. The disputed question of the fate of northern Ireland was met by the expedient of a 'temporary' partition which was to be resolved by negotiation. In the event, the partition hardened into permanent rigidity. In reply, the southern Irish systematically dismantled all that remained of the ties with England and eventually transformed Eire into a republic outside the Commonwealth.

Neither the family relationship with New Zealand and Australia nor the love-hate relationship with Ireland formed much of a guide to the future relations between Britain and the Indian sub-continent, after the second world war. There were so many questions to which the answer was unknown. First, was Britain in earnest about offering full self-government? Ever since 1920, Indians had been offered opportunities to govern themselves. But always, when things became difficult, Britain took over, and the Indian politicians were sent off to cool their heels. It was like a nursery tea party, where the children were encouraged to play the part of adults: but when the game became too noisy, nurse intervened and packed them off to bed. When the transfer of power to Indian hands had

begun in 1920, with partial provincial ministerial responsibility under Dyarchy, who could possibly have supposed
that Britain would still be in full control a quarter of a
century later? In 1945, would it be the same story over
again? And even if Britain was in earnest, would the offer
of self-government be unconditional? Or, as in the 1935
Government of India Act, would Britain insert those
'safeguards' which would ensure that Britain could return
to put the clock back if need be? Obviously, Newfoundland
was a special case; but some must have noted how, when
things went wrong in the 1930s in the oldest Dominion in
the Commonwealth, Britain went back. Would Britain
hand over a going concern to the new regime: or would
Britain pull out its administrative and commercial organization from India, leaving the new leaders to build up *ab
initio*? Would the British genuinely assist the newly
emerging nation to choose its own leaders and its own
institutions: or would they try to leave behind a Trojan
Horse? For example, in India would they manoeuvre
the Princes into a position of holding the balance of power
in the new state?

The denouement

When the play had at last been acted out, it was seen
that Britain really had intended to promote genuine, unfettered independence, and to do everything possible to
get things off to a good start. The effect of this denouement
on the subsequent unfolding of British decolonization was
enormous. There were disputes and difficulties, but seldom
was there a fog of mistrust and misunderstanding shroud-
ing the dealings between the British government (of
whichever complexion) and the national leaders.[2] Even

[2] Cyprus and Rhodesia provide two exceptions to this dictum. But it may
well be argued that in neither of these cases had the rulers or the people
formulated even a rudimentary definition of the precise goal at which they
were aiming.

where, as in Kenya, a gulf yawned between departing
rulers and emerging people, the transfer could be carried
out by agreement. What one may call the Lancaster House
pattern of independence-making by conference was made
possible by the pioneer experiment of bringing freedom to
India and Pakistan.

The aim of this brief essay is to attempt to re-create the
atmosphere of 1945-7 as it seemed at the time; and to try
to present the problems as they appeared before the
solutions had been devised. Some studies of this transfer of
power have suggested that the Labour government and
Lord Wavell as Viceroy frittered away more than eighteen
months in a fruitless attempt to secure a settlement, and
then in a kind of panic turned to Lord Mountbatten, who
scrambled through a half-baked solution to the problem.
It is the thesis of this essay that the two years from the
Simla conference to the final transfer form a whole: a
period in which it was necessary to 'sweat it out', remorse-
lessly to follow through all the alternatives, so that in the
end all parties were agreed that the final solution was
indeed the only possible, practicable solution. In this
long-drawn-out process, much time and attention had to
be given to questions which, in the end, became mere
side-issues, or even disappeared from view. Conversely,
problems loomed up in the last months or weeks before
independence which had not been anticipated in earlier
planning. To try to see these matters in their contemporary
setting is to acquire a more balanced understanding of
why the transfer of power worked out as it did.

In seeking to reinvoke these events—so near in time, yet
so divorced from the world in which we now live—the
author is quite frankly setting out what he sees as the last
chapter of a story of British imperial achievement: and
what might have been—but was not to be—the first
chapter of a new era of Commonwealth co-operation. The

Britain of 1945–7 was, like the Britain of today, playing an international role from a position of weakness. Yet this position of weakness was not accepted as sufficient reason for abandoning the effort to exercise a role. Britain's position in India had never depended upon brute strength, but upon an exertion of will by a relatively small body of Englishmen. At the last, when the British will-power appeared to be failing, there was a final act of will by the Viceroy of India and the government in Whitehall, supported by hundreds of British civil and military officers throughout the subcontinent. By this act of will, Britain played a full part, along with national leaders, in ushering out the old order and bringing in the new. Acts of will are rare in the Britain of the 1960s and this deserves to be recorded.

Retelling the story

These views of mine have not been held since the events under discussion occurred. Rather, they have formed in my mind as a result of an entirely fresh approach to the subject when, early in 1965, Professor C. H. Philips, Director of the School of Oriental and African Studies, decided to initiate a two-year seminar programme to re-examine the period leading up to the transfer of power. In this connexion, and also independently, I have had the opportunity to look at many of the materials and meet some of the men at the centre of the story. The dilemma which arises is whether or not to make direct use of the evidence so obtained, and whether or not to cite authority for this evidence. Two studies of recent years have applied two different sets of rules. Mr Michael Edwardes, in the Preface to *The Last Years of British India* (1963), is content to observe that 'Much of the real material of such history [contemporary history] is not, at least officially, available

to the historian'. He goes on to say that he has 'taken
every opportunity of checking the statements of individuals': and he leaves the matter at that. Mr Leonard
Mosley, author of *The Last Days of the British Raj* (1961), lists
the names of persons who have given him information in
his Preface, and in a number of footnotes indicates that he
is quoting from confidential documents. On occasion he
relates what is clearly a narrative by a participant in the
story. This technique gives the reader the opportunity to
evaluate the account by reference to sources: and is, of
course, standard practice among historians. However, I
have chosen to follow the same course as Mr Edwardes
and to present my narrative without any sort of corroboration from sources other than those which have appeared in print in some form. Public men, looking back at
the events in which they played a part, are often ready to
confide in somebody like myself who occupies a role of
(more or less) academic detachment. But they are unlikely
to give their confidence to someone who is liable to start
revealing names. Our knowledge of the events of 1945–7
depends in part at any rate upon such memories. One
distinguished Indian spectator of those days has told me
that it is very doubtful whether any of the front-rank
Indian leaders kept private papers: and some of the key
decisions are recorded only in memories.

However, there is a strong case for opening up the files
now for historians to work from the British documents
without further delay. First, this is an episode of history
to which FINIS has long been written, so far as British
policy is concerned. One can imagine other constitutional
episodes—such as the formation of the Central African
Federation—which will leave ripples across contemporary
politics for many decades. But 1947 marked the final end
of the long British policy-making effort in India: and an
honourable end it was. This is a cupboard without skele-

tons, and it can be opened without disturbing anything but the truth. Secondly, as in so many aspects of contemporary history, security has already been breached on a large scale. Mr V. P. Menon, in *The Transfer of Power in India* (1957), quotes upon almost every page, or else paraphrases, from documents which were originally classified as Top Secret. However, Mr Menon's discretion need not be questioned. Discussions which it was essential to keep secret before a final decision was taken or the final agreement clinched became matters of general interest before many years elapsed. Nevertheless, although Mr Menon's objectivity is not in question, like every historian he has to be selective in choosing the sources which he 'leaks' to us. Others are passed over, and so certain aspects of the story have not been given adequate emphasis. The case for selecting certain episodes of 'peacetime' history which fall within the fifty-year rule (or the thirty-year rule, as it may soon become) and opening these for scholarly examination—a possibility which the Prime Minister touched upon in a statement to the House of Commons on 9 March 1966—seems to apply without reservation to the papers relating to the transfer of power which at present lie unseen in the old India Office Records.

Meanwhile, this essay makes an attempt to elucidate and interpret the main themes of British policy, in relation to the objectives of the Congress and the Muslim League. Those who ask for proof for the statements that follow may first care to weigh the narrative in terms of its internal consistency. Then they will observe that corroboration is furnished by the various White Papers and by Mr Menon's *Transfer of Power*: although some aspects to which importance is given in this essay occur *en passant* in Menon. The careful reader will notice that in one important respect this essay departs from Mr Menon's version of a vital episode.

2

The British Approach to
Indian Self-Government

THE British approach to the question of self-government
for India began by looking for means to provide the
right kind of administration for a vast country and population over which the dome of British authority had been so
strenuously extended. From the 1870s there were attempts
at devolution, of which the partition of Bengal in 1905 is a
notorious example. The administrative requirement of
decentralization became merged into a political search for
means to extend Indian self-government. The first attempt
was Ripon's development of local self-government in the
1880s. After the unrest in Bengal and Maharashtra in the
early 1900s the problem became more urgent, and we find
the Viceroy writing in a dispatch to the Secretary of State
in August 1911:

> The only possible solution . . . would appear to be gradually
> to give the Provinces a larger measure of self-government,
> until at last India would consist of a number of administrations,
> autonomous in all provincial affairs, with the Government of
> India above them all.[1]

This conception of the provinces as the proving-ground of
Indian political responsibility was implemented in the
Montagu–Chelmsford 'Dyarchy' scheme of 1919, where-
by at the provincial level Indian politicians assumed

[1] C. H. Philips, ed., *The Evolution of India and Pakistan, 1858 to 1947*
1962), p. 91.

responsibility for the 'nation-building subjects', such as
education, health, local government, agriculture. Finally,
under the 1935 Government of India Act, the whole
sphere of provincial government was handed over to
ministers responsible to their provincial legislatures.

Community and nation

The other major question with which British policy was
concerned was to create a balanced relationship between
the different classes, communities, and creeds of India.
When representative institutions were established, the men
who emerged as political leaders belonged (as was natural)
to the *avant garde*, the professional middle class: mainly
lawyers, mainly Hindus of the literary castes. British policy
sought to balance this representation of what was called a
'microscopic minority' by bringing forward the Princes,
the aristocracy, the gentry, members of the non-literary
castes—and the Muslims. Under the Morley–Minto reforms of 1909, the device of Separate Electorates was
inserted into the nascent system of representation. British
public men expressed many reservations about this
development, so obviously calculated to emphasize differences within the community. But once set out on this road
it was hard to turn back. The Montagu–Chelmsford reforms reluctantly continued the system. There were signs
that the Indian political leaders understood the importance
of bridging the differences between communities and
classes: and so a British policy line emerged. The Indian
leaders must combine to resolve their differences: only
then could self-government become a reality. What was
underlying this line of policy? Was it intended to provide
an incentive to the different parties in Indian politics to
come together? Or was it a device to postpone *sine die* the
development of self-government by encouraging the rivals

to bargain and manoeuvre to obtain the best terms for their own special interest?

Indian political leaders began to react actively to the self-government trend of British policy. Those with a vested interest in the *status quo*, especially the Princes and the aristocrats, began to mount a long rearguard action designed to resist change. Those who thought of themselves as underprivileged minorities—like the lower castes and the main body of the Muslims—began to agitate for constitutional devices to provide a recognized place for their community under any reforms. But some Muslims saw their role in the future as participation in a national movement. At an auspicious hour, when the world was talking of democracy and national self-determination, these progressive Muslims met their counterparts in the Indian National Congress at Lucknow in 1916. Together they agreed that, for the time being, the system of separate electorates for Muslims must be accepted until communal differences had been resolved. Many of these Muslims came from the United Provinces and Bombay, where their community formed a small minority of the total population; therefore they concentrated on securing a recognized position for themselves as one element in the political spectrum. In two of the most important provinces, Bengal and Punjab, the Muslims were actually in a majority. Previously, this had been of little consequence as the highly selective municipal franchise, based on property qualifications, had given the Hindu middle class a controlling voice. Under the Lucknow Pact the Muslims in the provinces where they formed minorities received a 'weightage' which gave them much greater representation than their population strength: in return, in Bengal and Punjab they conceded a greater representation to the non-Muslims. In consequence, despite their numerical superiority in these provinces, the Muslims signed away their potential capacity to call the political tune in the north west and the east of India.

Of course, this is to envisage politics in terms of crude communalism. The architects of the Lucknow Pact had the vision to look beyond communal politics: their purpose was to build into the system such safeguards as would permit the different communities to be assured about their position *vis-à-vis* each other, and so move forward together in a movement for national self-government. This was the spirit pervading Indian politics for the next decade. But when the virus of communalism became all-pervasive twenty years later, the Muslims were to discover that they had lost control over their strongholds, the Muslim-majority provinces.

The Congress, and party politics

The settlement negotiated in the Lucknow Pact was introduced into the Dyarchy reforms of 1919 which created territorial constituencies for the first time. Besides the 'general' constituencies (actually those for the Hindu population) there were special constituencies—also on a territorial basis—for Muslims, and Sikhs in Punjab, as well as for smaller communities like Indian Christians and Anglo-Indians. This electoral system tended to produce a political situation in which individual leaders or local groups secured election, and then entered into a combination to which they gave a party label. In two provinces local political movements emerged with some of the characteristics of a party: the Justice Party in Madras and the Unionists of Punjab. The Justice Party represented the protest of the non-Brahmins against Brahmin dominance in South India. The Unionist Party was a grouping of rural interests; the leading element being the Muslim landlords of west Punjab, associated with Sikh rural leaders and the Jats of east Punjab. Both these provincial parties had a distinct programme, some kind of organization in the districts, and a cohesive group, acting together, in the legislature. The Congress remained as the only all-India party, with a distinct constitution and organization and regular party conferences to consider and endorse a political programme. However, the leaders of the Congress from 1920 down to 1935 could not agree on committing the movement to participating in the provincial legislatures and ministries. Attempts by the Congress to follow the revolutionary American and Irish examples, and set up a parallel political system in defiance of the British Raj (attempts which reached their climax in the Lahore 'Declaration of Independence' in 1929) could not be pressed home largely because of the bourgeois character of the active membership of the Congress. So many of the lawyers, journalists, and teachers who filled its ranks fulfilled a parasitic role in relation to the apparatus of British government. Their leaders were prepared to go to jail; the rank and file were ready to participate in processions and agitations; but they were not prepared to give up their professional relationships with the courts and the colleges of the British for a revolutionary struggle. Moreover, the strength of the Congress varied considerably in different parts of India. It *did* have the rudiments of organization everywhere, but only in the Gangetic heartland and in the areas of Gujarat where the Patel brothers' writ ran was the Congress able effectively to mobilize mass support.

However, the British were too inclined in the 1920s and 1930s to regard the Congress as the extremist section of Indian political life, failing to recognize that it represented the main body of progressive and moderate opinion in India. By contrast, the Muslim League in the 1920s was reduced to a nominal existence. In its early days it had

been a suitable vehicle for making representations to the
British authorities, but it had never developed from a
pressure group into a party. With the more enterprising
Muslim politicians co-operating with the Congress, the
League wilted. The outstanding Muslim politician,
Mohammed Ali Jinnah, left Indian politics to practise law
in London.

Conferring and constitution-making

When the British government summoned a Round
Table Conference in London in 1931, to deliberate on
constitutional reform, they issued invitations to almost
every conceivable group and community to send representatives. The conference somewhat resembled the *darbar*
of an Indian prince, where all classes and interests have
their recognized place. To this *omnium gatherum* the Congress
chose to nominate one representative only, Gandhi. This
served further to mask the growing political reality—that
Congress was the only organized political party in India—
and to concede weight to distinguished individuals, like
the Indian liberals, who in reality could 'deliver' nothing
except themselves. The Conference was invited to reach
agreement upon its own terms for the future government
of India. Before the advent of Gandhi, they agreed upon a
federal form of government in which the centre would
retain a relatively limited range of responsibilities. But the
second session, which Gandhi attended, was unable to
settle the question of representation: because the various
minorities insisted that their separate claims must be given
constitutional recognition. As no agreement could be
reached, the Prime Minister (Ramsay MacDonald) issued
a 'Communal Award' which laid down the numbers of
seats which would be reserved for the Muslims, Sikhs, and
other minorities.[2] This preserved the Lucknow Pact prin-

[2] *East India (Constitutional Reforms) Communal Decision.* Cmd. 4147 (1932).

ciple of 'weightage', and also gave the Muslims a third of the seats in the central legislature: a greater proportion than their place in the population (one-quarter) would have given.

These provisions were embodied in the 1935 Government of India Act. The rules for transferring power in India which appeared to be evolving were as follows: the British government would consult all shades of Indian opinion on the terms of constitutional advance; where agreement was reached among Indians, the British government would accept this as the basis for change; where no agreement could be reached, the British government would act as arbiter and impose an award; the reforms would be implemented through legislation of the British parliament.

When elections were held under the extended franchise of the 1935 Act, early in 1937, the Congress obtained a clear majority in five of the eleven provinces. After some debate, the Congress formed ministries in six provinces. The 'bandwagon' began to gather momentum. Politicians began to adhere to the party which looked like dominating Indian politics in the future. Congress was able to form ministries in two further provinces as a result of further support: these were in the North-West Frontier Province, overwhelmingly Muslim, and in Assam, with a bare Muslim majority.

The Muslim League had made a poor showing in the 1937 elections, winning only 108 of the 482 seats reserved for Muslims at the provincial level. This compared with 716 seats won by Congress out of the overall provincial total of 1,585 (i.e. including the 'reserved' constituencies). The Congress triumph was a little marred by their gaining only 26 of the Muslim seats. The main successes of the League were in the minority provinces: Bombay, Madras, and the United Provinces. They also won 39 out of the 117

Muslim seats in Bengal, but in Punjab, Sind, and the NWFP they could only take a total of four seats (combined Muslim seats in these three provinces numbered 153). The feebleness of this result must be set against the situation of the hour. The Muslim political ranks were hopelessly divided in the mid-1930s. Jinnah returned to India after many years in London only in 1935, and the 1937 elections were fought after only a few months' effort had been put into flinging together a scratch organization. Their relative failure acted as a spur to the Muslim leaders.

The split between Congress and Muslim League

One incident in the United Provinces was to have protracted repercussions. There the Muslim League was mainly composed of members, or former members, of the Congress, and they understood that after the election there would be a common front.[3] When Congress came to form a ministry, they told the League leaders that they would be offered posts only on condition that they joined the Congress and accepted its rulings. These terms were refused, and an immediate trial of strength was sought in a fiercely contested by-election in a UP Muslim constituency, which the League won. The incident demonstrated that the Congress was not prepared to accept situations of compromise, to be resolved by coalitions or agreements. Adherents would only be accepted upon Congress's terms. The incident also demonstrated the capacity of the League to fight back when rebuffed, and to call upon the latent sense of 'Islam in danger' which would appeal more than any other political slogan to the Muslim community.

The transfer of power to elected ministries at the provincial level was intended to be only one feature of the

[3] The nature of this understanding has been much disputed. Jinnah was not in favour of a Congress–League alliance.

1935 reforms. Of even greater consequence was to be the formation of a federal superstructure, as the first step in bringing the princely states and British India into one political system. But despite their earlier support for federation, the Princes decided to postpone their adherence to the new constitution: and so, at the all-India level, the limited constitution of the Dyarchy period continued. While, in the provinces, effective political power had passed from the hands of officials to Indian politicians, at the centre the Raj continued to function at the behest of the Viceroy. This tended to create a feeling that while constitutional deadlock prevailed at the centre, the provinces were 'going concerns' where political initiative was being exercised and might develop further.

Within the British government, on the eve of war there was a general recognition that the 1935 Act represented the last stage upon the road to self-government. However, Dyarchy had persisted for nearly two decades, and another twenty might elapse before full self-government was attained. Perhaps because the British Empire was already, in a sense, an 'imperial museum', there was little interest in India within the Cabinet, despite the presence of Halifax and Hoare, as well as Zetland: all men with a desire to see constitutional advance and agreement.[4] There was less awareness of the passage of time in the Government of India, where the Viceroy, Lord Linlithgow, found an obstacle for every solution.

War and political realignments

The outbreak of war quickened the pulse of thinking in the India Office a little. It was realized that the churning-up of so many accepted institutions and ideas would result

---

[4] Halifax was a former Viceroy; Hoare, the previous Secretary of State; Zetland, Secretary of State, 1937–40.

in a new situation in which India might move rapidly towards Dominion status. However, any such tendency towards meeting Indian opinion was overtaken by the decision of the Congress High Command to order the provincial Congress ministries to vacate office, following the unilateral commitment of India to the war effort by the Viceroy, on behalf of the British government. This move was not taken without opposition from the Congress moderates (notably Rajagopalachari, the Premier of Madras) but once put into effect this reversed the trend begun in 1937 to convert the Congress into a constitutional, co-operative movement. Subsequently a pure Gandhian policy was adopted. Individuals were asked to perform *satyagraha* or symbolic acts of civil disobedience. Gandhi had learnt through experience that mass *satyagraha* could degenerate into violence and mob action. And so he was content to invoke the actions of a few to remind the British government that it did not enjoy the support of the Congress. After the resignation of the eight Congress ministries, provincial administration became the direct responsibility of the British Governor under the provisions of Section 93 of the Government of India Act. Leading Congressmen were taken into custody as political prisoners. Doubtless many British officials were relieved to be able to devote their full energies to mobilizing India's men and resources for the war, without being compelled to follow the instructions of Congress politicians.

Meanwhile the Muslim League stepped into the political vacuum. In March 1940, at their annual meeting in Lahore, the League adopted a resolution calling for the creation of 'independent states' in the north-western and eastern zones of India. Jinnah declared that Hindus and Muslims were 'two nations' and the Muslims must have 'their homelands, their territory and their state'.

There was nothing novel in any of these propositions.

For seventy years, such ideas had been invoked, never quite specifically formulated and defined, in the minds of Muslim leaders. Jinnah had never been associated with such demands: indeed, he had insisted that he was a nationalist, first and last. But while he felt at home in the old Congress of liberal principles and constitutional methods, he had become alienated from a Congress which he believed was neo-Hindu, authoritarian, and non-constitutional; the Congress of Gandhi and Nehru. Between 1935 and 1940 he seems to have come to feel that the Congress intended the destruction of the League and the subordination of the Muslims. Therefore it was vital that the Muslims should have their own strongholds, Cities of Refuge, wherein they would be inviolable. Because the only respectable political vocabulary for peoples demanding freedom was the vocabulary of nationalism, the Muslim League spoke in terms of a Muslim nation. But the 1940 resolution leaves it open for the interpreter to decide whether the demand was for autonomy within, or without some form of all-India union. The Lahore resolution demanded that

geographically contiguous units are demarcated into regions which should be so constituted with such territorial readjustments as may be necessary that the areas in which the Muslims are numerically in a majority, as in the north-western and eastern zones of India, should be grouped to constitute 'independent states' in which the constituent units shall be autonomous and sovereign.[5]

If there was any ambiguity about this phrasing it was obliterated by the press, which promptly dubbed this the 'Pakistan resolution', adopting the name of a scheme devised by an Indian Muslim living in Cambridge. Pakistan: this was the name which gave the breath of life to the arid phrases of a party resolution. Pakistan: this

[5] Philips, pp. 345–6.

was the talking-point of Indian politics from that day
forward. Probably without realising their achievement,
the League leaders had wrested the initiative from the
hands of the Congress High Command. Henceforward
any constitutional discussion had to begin by considering
the merits or demerits of Pakistan.[6]

British opinion was almost unanimous in declaring that
the 'Pakistan demand' was a deliberate over-bid by the
League to obtain full consideration for the Muslim point
of view in the final reckoning. Some British officials wel
comed this plan as a means of check-mating Congress'
demands; the majority dismissed it with incredulity. What
they demanded, would happen to the great centres of the
Muslim tradition, Delhi, Lucknow, and Hyderabad? They
would be lost to Pakistan: indeed, those most in favour of
the scheme, the Muslims of the minority provinces, stood
to gain nothing by its introduction. Having thus disposed
of Pakistan, the mass of observers went on to speculate
about what Jinnah really wanted: but still it was
Jinnah that they looked for the key.

A change was coming over British policy towards India
at the highest level. After the formation of a coalition
government in 1940, Leo Amery became Secretary of
State. A number of Cabinet committees were formed in
1942, in order to free the inner Cabinet. Policy-making for
India was entrusted to a committee of the Cabinet, the
India Committee, whose chairman was C. R. Attlee, the
deputy Prime Minister. Other members were Amery, Sir
John Anderson, Sir P. J. Grigg, and Sir Stafford Cripps.[7]
Thinking on the India Committee was in favour of early
self-government for India, but from Delhi came only the
most cautious response from the Viceroy.

[6] The League officially adopted Pakistan as the goal only in April 946.
[7] Anderson had been Governor of Bengal; Grigg had been a member of
the Viceroy's Council.

The Cripps mission

After the entry of Japan into the war, and the invasion of Malaya and Burma, the Committee gave urgent consideration to means whereby Indian political leadership could be associated with the war effort. One proposal was for an advisory council to provide moral support for the defence of India; this council might, after the war ended, become a constitution-making body. The Viceroy objected to a plan which would confuse two objectives; so as an alternative the India Committee proposed issuing a declaration of policy. This would concede to India the right of secession from the Empire, and announce the intention of setting up a constitution-making body, to be elected by the provincial legislatures (after they had been given a mandate by fresh elections). This body would devise a constitution for an Indian Union; provinces which might decline to join might exercise 'local option' to defer their adherence to the Union. The new India would enter a new relationship with the United Kingdom by means of a treaty.

The provision for 'local option', the right to exercise a choice whether to come in or stay out of the Union, followed the terms of the 1935 Act with regard to the setting up of a federation, whereby the princely states were permitted to exercise a similar option. Cripps then suggested that if he could fly to India to convey these proposals to the Indian leaders this might offer a better prospect of acceptance. After some delay, Cripps left England in 1-March 1942, arriving in India on 23 March.

There was a precedent for the Cripps mission in the visit Edwin Montagu to India which laid the basis for the tagu–Chelmsford reforms. However, the new feature is visit lay in the approach from the rulers to the . Cripps was to place the British proposals before the

Indian leaders, while the eventual process of constitution-making was envisaged as being carried through by the Indians themselves: the British role being confined to ratifying the new constitutional set-up by treaty. The main work of nation-making was, henceforth, to be transferred from Westminster to New Delhi.

Soon after Cripps arrived, the main features of the scheme became the subject of rumour, so a declaration was issued on 30 March outlining the plan. The procedure for creating a new constitution by Constituent Assembly was formulated, 'subject only to the right of any Province of British India that is not prepared to accept the new Constitution to retain its present constitutional position, provision being made for its subsequent accession if it so decides'. The procedure for a Constituent Assembly met the requirements of accepted Congress policy; however, an addendum gave an indication of inching a little towards Pakistan: 'His Majesty's Government will be prepared to agree upon a new constitution, giving them [the non-acceding provinces] the same full status as the Indian Union'.

The League indicated that if the Congress would accept the scheme, they would do the same, but the Congress leaders proved obdurate. The promise of future freedom was balanced by insistence upon immediate support in defence. Despite pressure from President Roosevelt's envoy, Colonel Louis Johnson, the Congress held out for an assurance that the Viceroy would accept a majority decision by his Executive Council. Cripps returned to London in mid-April, his mission a failure.[8]

Soon after the Cripps mission, Churchill surprised King George VI by declaring 'that his colleagues and both or all three parties in Parliament were quite prepared to

---

[8] *India (Lord Privy Seal's Mission), Statement and Draft Declaration by HMG, with correspondence and resolutions connected therewith.* Cmd. 6350 (1942).

give up India to the Indians after the war. He felt that they had already been talked into giving up India.'[9] But the next turn of events was to make any negotiation with the Indian political leaders more remote than ever.

Do or die

By June 1942 the Japanese forces had swept forward to the eastern frontier of India, and only the deluge of the monsoon prevented further advance. The Japanese navy threatened the coastline from Madras to Calcutta. Faced with the likelihood of Japanese invasion, Gandhi led the Congress in a demand to the British to Quit India. On 7 August the All-India Congress Committee met under Gandhi's leadership. The immediate departure of the British was demanded: if this were refused then there would follow 'a mass struggle on non-violent lines on the widest possible scale'. The British reply was to arrest Gandhi and the Working Committee on 9 August. Perhaps Gandhi may have intended the struggle to be non-violent: but the militant sections of the Congress which had been preparing for a show-down made plans for the exercise of physical force. For example, the Engineering College at the Banaras Hindu University had trained its students in the techniques of sabotage. The Congress slogan was *Karenge Ya Marenge*, 'Let us Do or Die'. The removal of Gandhi meant that leadership was in the hands of the younger men of the Left Wing, such as Jayaprakash Narayan.[10] In the course of the rising, communications between northern and eastern India were totally disrupted, and several districts in the

[9] J. W. Wheeler-Bennett, *King George VI; his life and reign* (1958), p. 703.
[10] Jayaprakash was jailed in March 1940, but he escaped in September 1942 and led the guerrilla campaign. He was captured in Nepal, escaped, and was finally arrested in Punjab in September 1943. He was not released from jail until 1946, long after the other leaders were set free.

Banaras Division of the UP, as well as most of Bihar, passed into Congress control. However, within six weeks the revolt was over, and all the leaders except a few fugitives were behind bars. For years militant Indian nationalists had talked about 1857 as the Indian War of Independence. August 1942 saw an all-out effort to wage a war of independence: and it failed. This failure must have been a bitter lesson to the Congress leaders. They saw that mass support for their movement was confined to the Congress heartland. They saw that the lawyers, students, and teachers who were their mainstay could successfully seize the headquarters of the District Magistrate, against the opposition of a police riot squad: but they could not oppose even the tail-end forces which the British scraped together in the hour of chaos which followed the retreat from Burma. Above all, they must have noted with special disillusionment that, with a few exceptions, the Muslim population held aloof from the struggle, even in UP and Bihar. The rising was accompanied by acts of bestial cruelty by some of the Congress mobs, while captured Congress leaders afterwards deposed that they were handled brutally by the police. The 'August Disturbances', as they were euphemistically called, marked the lowest point in British-Indian relations. All communication seemed to be severed. Only bitterness and suspicion remained.[11]

The August Disturbances left a legacy of misapprehensions on all sides. The British mistakenly saw them as the first round in a coming struggle by force. They characterized the Congress as an extremist, revolutionary organization; using the moderate men as a front, but basically committed to a programme of violence. Gandhi was envisaged as a kind of Mephistopheles, blandly

[11] *India: Statement by the Government of India on the Congress Party's Responsibility for the disturbances in India, 1942–1943.* Cmd. 6430 (1943).

speaking honeyed words while preparing evil deeds. Nehru was suspected as a confirmed revolutionary, while Jayaprakash was regarded as the coming leader, the guerrilla captain who would take over when the talking stopped.

Perhaps because they had failed, the Congress leaders unduly elevated the significance of their struggle and sacrifice: they alone were the Freedom Fighters, entitled to represent India, while those who had stood aside—especially the League—were parlour politicians, creatures of the British, unfit to speak for the people.

Wavell: the soldier administrator

For two years there was silence in Indian politics. Linlithgow was replaced in October 1943 by Wavell, previously Commander-in-Chief, India. Son of a family of soldiers, Wavell recognized as early as the Curragh 'Mutiny' that the duty of the soldier is to obey the civil power. After a brilliant period as Chief of Staff to Allenby in the Palestine campaign, Wavell languished through the twenty years of peace in relatively unimportant posts, until suddenly raised to high position in the late 1930's. From 1937 he dealt with a mounting succession of crises as Commander-in-Chief in the Middle East, almost always finding himself denied adequate resources. Faced with the constant possibility of having to fend for himself as best he could, Wavell maintained a file labelled 'Worst Possible Case', designed to provide contingency planning for emergencies. An incisive intellect was concealed behind a taciturn countenance, and only a devoted few aroused from Wavell more than the gruff 'I see' which was his response to most efforts at communication.

Wavell took over as Viceroy in the familiar atmosphere of crisis: the agonies of the Bengal famine. If anything, this further strained relations between Indians and British, as the allegation was made that the famine had been permitted because foodgrains had been diverted from the civil population to military use. However, Wavell was as determined to discover a political initiative as his predecessor had been to discourage any new venture. The middle years of the war saw the consolidation of the Muslim League in the Muslim-majority provinces. League politicians were able to take advantage of the eclipse of Congress to form ministries in Assam, Sind, and the North-West Frontier, while in Bengal the most loyal League supporter, Nazimuddin, became Premier. Only Punjab eluded Jinnah's control. The Unionist Party had been led by two men of stature, Fazl-i-Husain and Sikander Hyat Khan. Both recognised the League as the national vehicle of the Muslims, but insisted that they held the reins in Punjab. Both men met untimely deaths. Sikander Hyat died in 1942, and his successor came from the ranks of the great landlords: a natural leader in former days, but not adapted to the new politics of manoeuvre. Wavell took a strong position on the Pakistan issue almost immediately. He insisted on the geographical unity of India, but equally he acknowledged the right of the Muslims to recognition of their special position. He re-emphasized the importance of the different parties in India meeting to compose their differences. Early in 1944 he made some contribution to easing the political log-jam by beginning to release the Congress leaders from confinement. Those who were adjudged the least extreme were released first, while the militants were still confined. A small section of the Congress leadership had already acknowledged that relations with the Muslim community had deteriorated to such a point that confidence could only be restored by conceding the Pakistan demand. Rajagopalachari had been expelled from Congress for advocating this policy early in 1942. In July 1944 he refined his proposals. After the war a commission should be appointed to demarcate the Muslim-majority areas in the north-west and east. There a plebiscite should be held to establish the wishes of the people, and if they desired they should be permitted to establish a separate polity, linked with the residual India only for defence, commerce, and communications. In a famous phrase Jinnah dismissed this proposal as offering only a 'maimed, mutilated and moth-eaten Pakistan'.[12] However, talks were arranged between Jinnah and Gandhi in September 1944. Gandhi was prepared to concede a great deal to give the Muslims autonomy in their majority areas: but he declined to acknowledge that the Muslims of India constituted a separate nation. Jinnah, on his side, stood out for the 'full' Pakistan of six provinces: Sind, Baluchistan, NWFP, and Punjab in the north-west, Bengal and Assam in the east. This ignored that passage in the Lahore resolution which mentioned 'such territorial readjustments as may be necessary', implying that the key provinces of Punjab and Bengal might have to shed the predominantly non-Muslim areas.

The Simla conference

The bid by the Indian leaders to resolve their differences was over. Wavell inferred that this might be the moment when British initiative would be welcomed. After preliminary exchanges, he flew to London, where he remained from 23 March to 1 June, 1945. A great deal was happening at this time. The war in Europe had ended. The British Labour and Liberal parties withdrew from the coalition and plans went ahead for a general election. At the same time, steps were taken to transfer

[12] V. P. Menon, *The Transfer of Power in India* (1957), p. 163.

British forces to the Far East in preparation for what was expected to be a long, country-by-country campaign to wear down Japan. In this phase of the war, India would play a vital part as a base and staging post.

Wavell suggested that a conference should be summoned to discuss the formation of an interim government on a popular basis to see through the war against Japan and to prepare for full self-government. The Viceroy was fortified by a parliamentary statement by Amery, indicating that the Cripps offer of terms for independence immediately hostilities ceased would still be honoured.[13]

On his return to Delhi, Wavell invited twenty-one political leaders to meet at Simla on 25 June. This was to be another *omnium gatherum* on Round Table Conference lines, but the principal dialogue was clearly to be that of Congress and League. Informal discussions between the two parties had thrown up the suggestion that there might be agreement that each should enjoy an equal share of posts on the Executive Council, with the remainder allotted to other minority interests. Although the Congress strenuously resisted the 'two-nations' concept, there was already a tacit agreement that the Muslims had ceased to be a minority, like the Sikhs, Parsis, or Indian Christians. The conference met at a time when the League appeared to have lost ground in the provinces, after the return of Congress detainees into the legislatures. Jinnah's response was to stiffen his conditions. When four portfolios on the Viceroy's Council were offered to the League, with one post going to a Unionist Muslim (a token of the major contribution to army recruiting made by Punjabis), Jinnah objected to any nominating of a Muslim except from the ranks of the League. Wavell refused to accept this ultimatum. At the same time he was not prepared to

[13] *India: Statement of the policy of HMG made by the Secretary of State for India on June 14th 1946.* Cmd. 6652.

overrule Jinnah and construct his Council without League co-operation. On 14 July the Viceroy announced that the conference had been unable to agree upon the composition of an interim government.

The Simla conference took place in the interregnum between the election in Britain and the announcement of the result. The timing had been disrupted by the onrush of events. Three weeks later the Emperor of Japan announced his country's surrender, while a Labour government with a massive majority came into power in Britain. It was a new world, offering a new opportunity in India: but all the old problems remained, to drag along, unsolved and apparently insoluble.

After the Simla conference, Wavell convened a meeting of all the Governors. They were unanimous in opposing the partition of India, while the Governor of the Punjab made it clear that the alternatives were either agreement on an Indian union—for which no formula acceptable to the League had been devised—or the partition of his province, and also that of Bengal.

The Labour government

Meanwhile the new Labour Cabinet had, amid all the problems of war and peace, hastened to replace the former coalition India Committee by an India–Burma Committee of the Cabinet. Attlee continued as the chairman, and Cripps remained a member. Lord Pethick-Lawrence, the new Secretary of State, was naturally included, while other ministers formed a kind of outer circle. These were Lord Stansgate (a former Secretary of State for India), Ellen Wilkinson, and Lord Listowel. Although India had not featured high in Labour's election manifesto, there was a clear determination to achieve self-government—which might mean independence outside the

Empire—as soon as possible. As a first step, it was decided to prepare the ground for provincial elections.

Wavell came to London for a series of discussions with the India Committee during the first half of September. As a soldier, he tried to establish the importance of rigorously defining the objectives. First, they must confront the possibility of Pakistan. Only by examining its implications would the parties in India be induced to abandon negative tactics. Only if the parties understood that Britain would see through to the end the task of securing agreement would India be preserved from misfortune. Perhaps Wavell, like many others, expected that the Labour government would apply a doctrinaire solution to the Indian problem; one that would favour the allegedly socialist Congress at the expense of more conservative elements. Indeed, it might appear surprising that a Labour government, returned for the first time with an absolute majority, would follow the same course as its predecessors: looking back at the steps already taken, comparing these with the claims of the parties in India, and searching for means to reconcile conflicts in a formula of agreement. Yet this was the course adopted—empirical, not theoretical—and the ministers went back to the Cripps formula as a starting point for their discussions.

Once again, the possibility was raised of the provinces desirous of framing a new constitution being invited to go ahead, while the reluctant provinces might remain under British rule, for the time being, and might as a last resort form a separate union. The exercise of 'local option' might give the Muslims better terms: but the alternative of coercing the Muslims was out of the question. Certainly the Committee was facing up to the difficult questions: but it was not discovering the answers.

Having returned to India, the Viceroy went ahead with preparations for the elections. The results of the voting

for the central legislative assembly were announced late
in December. The franchise was limited, favouring
conservative candidates. The League won all the seats
reserved for Muslims, while the Congress was the only
party represented from the general constituencies (there
were five independents). The contest was, indeed, now
between Congress and League alone.

Court martial and mutiny

Also, at the end of 1945, British prestige took its first
fall with the miserable muddle of the trials of the leaders
of the Japanese-sponsored Indian National Army. This
force, recruited partly from captured Indian prisoners
of war, had contained a number of bad officers who had
behaved brutally to their own countrymen. GHQ India
chose for the publicized court martial in the Red Fort at
Delhi three young officers who were notably inspired by
patriotic (if misguided) motives. Moreover they selected
a Hindu, a Muslim, and a Sikh. For the last time, all the
political leaders were united. Both Nehru and Jinnah
appeared as counsel for the defence. We need not follow
through the proceedings to the final anti-climax; sufficient to say that many British civil and military officers
began to doubt the political *savoir-faire* of their seniors,
while morale in the ranks of the Indian army was severely
shaken. Against this background, the Viceroy formulated
his post-election programme. He would bring together a
new Executive Council of Indian members, and ask them
to consider proposals for constitutional reform, which
would then be passed to a full constitutional conference.
In case Jinnah did not agree, he would be told that he
could have a Pakistan composed of the actual Muslim-
majority areas: the areas which were eventually to
become Pakistan. Wavell believed that, confronted by the

implications of a 'moth-eaten' Pakistan—shorn of Calcutta, and deprived of perhaps half Punjab and Bengal—Jinnah would accept an alternative solution.

Pethick-Lawrence told his colleagues that the Viceroy's plan for a partition was the most fair that could be devised. However, the Cabinet baulked at giving its assent to a programme which might, without further deliberation, lead to the division of India. On top of the Viceroy's 'breakdown' plan came the results of the provincial elections.[14] These followed the same pattern. The League won 439 out of the total of 494 seats reserved for Muslims, up and down India. This time the Muslim-majority provinces also voted solidly for League candidates: except in the North-West Frontier, where the pro-Congress Red Shirts won 19 out of the 38 Muslim seats. The Congress swamped all rival parties in the general constituencies, regaining its hold over Assam, the UP, Bihar, the Central Provinces, Orissa, Bombay, and Madras. In Punjab the Congress made gains at the expense of the Unionists, but the communal balance of forces left no party in a commanding situation.

While the lines were being drawn by the peoples of India, a further episode emphasized the failing power of the British to enforce control over events, as in the past. Towards the end of 1945, there had been mutinies among RAF personnel, idle and discontented with Indian conditions. These mutinies had been treated as 'strikes' and the superior authorities had acceded to their demands. On 18 February, units of the Royal Indian Navy went 'on strike' in imitation, formulating their demands which were backed by threats to use their guns on civil targets. The party leaders had given all support to the INA

---

[14] About 30 per cent. of the adult population were enfranchised. The percentage was higher among the upper castes, and much lower among the untouchables.

leaders; now they realized that there was danger in encouraging the armed forces to throw off their loyalty, even to the British Crown. A rebellious military might one day turn against them. And so Congress leaders—especially Vallabhbhai Patel—used their influence to induce the naval ratings to give in. The naval mutiny at Bombay lasted for five days: on its second day (19 February) the Prime Minister announced that a Cabinet delegation would come out to India to meet the political leaders in order to attempt to find a solution to the future constitutional evolution of India.

3

The Cabinet Mission Devise a Scheme
(March-May 1946)

THE Cabinet Mission consisted of three ministers: Pethick-Lawrence, Cripps, and A. V. Alexander, First Lord of the Admiralty, and later Minister of Defence. Long before his appointment as Secretary of State, Pethick-Lawrence had been a friend of India, and had visited the country. Now an old man, he had a sweet nature but an austere personality, shaped by his religion: his was a character to appeal to Gandhi, and leaders of his persuasion. Cripps was, of course, regarded as the pacemaker. An advocate of great persuasive power and ingenuity, he was an ardent socialist, and a man of strong likes and dislikes. Always at work devising new initiatives, his physical constitution was unequal to the strain he placed upon it, and illness lurked at his side. Alexander had been included in the Mission because of the defence implications of handing over the central bastion of Imperial defences in the Indian Ocean area to national leaders. As a Service minister, Alexander had the reputation of responding over-much to dynamic commanders. He came to India, as he said, without having formulated presuppositions or prejudices. The three ministers were joined in their endeavours by the Viceroy, who participated in all their decisions and was for all purposes a fourth member of the Mission. Wavell's personal relations with the ministers varied. Between him and Pethick-Lawrence there was mutual respect, and the Secretary of State paid full attention to the authority which the Viceroy (drawing upon the entire Indian administration) brought to every problem. Between Wavell and Cripps, a certain lack of rapport had already appeared, and was to grow. Alexander came to hold an admiration for Wavell amounting almost to hero-worship, which prevailed even though he came to follow a different line and policy.

Between the three ministers there was a close relationship, even if Pethick-Lawrence naturally regarded Cripps's assumption of leadership with a certain reserve.[1] They occupied their own quarters, at a distance from the Viceroy's house, and while Wavell maintained the aloofness traditional to his state, the ministers were accessible at all hours to any who wanted to see them. This was the special feature of the Cabinet Mission: they negotiated with the party leaders on terms of complete equality and considerable informality. There was no question of misunderstanding arising because of lack of direct and equal communication.

Before leaving England, the Mission discussed their terms of reference. They would try to by-pass the Pakistan issue and seek a 'confederal' solution, in which Pakistan, Hindustan, and some of the major princely states might become confederal units.[2] In forming an interim government, the formula of equal representation of Congress and the League would be followed: with additional representation of the Scheduled Castes. But in general their approach would be to assist the Indian leaders to find their own solutions, coming forward with concrete

[1] The Secretary of State wrote to his wife: 'Sir Stafford Cripps is like the dove that Noah sent out from the Ark. He is constantly going out making contacts, but up till now finding no solid ground' (Vera Brittain, *Pethick-Lawrence; a Portrait* (1963), p. 155).

[2] 'Hindustan' was used as a shorthand term for India, less Pakistan, right down to partition.

proposals only if the leaders failed to reach agreement. It was an optimistic reading of the situation, and Wavell lost no time in reminding them that far from shelving the Pakistan issue, this was the main hurdle to be taken. Congress resolutions had declared that the Muslims would not be forced into an Indian Union if this was against their will: but equally the non-Muslims of Punjab and Bengal could not be compelled to enter Pakistan against their will. If Jinnah maintained his demand for the full six-provinces Pakistan, how far was the Mission prepared to adjudicate on the question of the partition of Punjab and Bengal?

The Mission began by a series of formal interviews with everybody of note, official, political, and commercial, throughout the land. Gandhi proved somewhat enigmatic. He was ready to concede to the Muslims independence of culture and a legitimate ambition: but the two-nation theory was far more dangerous. To avoid an exhausting struggle, Gandhi suggested that Jinnah should be invited to form the government, choosing his members from elected representatives. There was, of course, the difficulty that a majority of the provincial legislatures owed allegiance to the Congress, but with goodwill a solution could be found. Very different was the attitude of Jinnah, etched in acid. He was insistent on the six provinces: there might be some territorial adjustments, but not over Calcutta, as necessary to Pakistan as the heart is to a man. Only the politicians on the fringes looked to the Cabinet Mission to issue an award to break the deadlock. The principal protagonists had their own ideas: which the Mission could not find reconcilable.

The first Cripps formula

It was left to Cripps to formulate proposals. He devised two alternatives. First, a scheme for a confederation, composed of Muslim provinces, Hindu provinces, and the princely states. The centre would have overall responsibility for defence, foreign relations, and communications. The central government would be drawn from the three components. In the beginning, three constituent assemblies would meet, followed by joint deliberations for a Union constitution. The second proposal was for 'Two Indias', Hindustan and Pakistan. There would be a partition in Punjab. The Two Indias would be associated for defence and foreign relations. These were both really projections of a strong (or medium) and weak form of confederation.

The main objection to this scheme came from the spokesmen on defence. Still thinking of the traditional watch and ward on the North-West Frontier, it was believed that Pakistan would not be equal to this task. A defence organization, linking the Two Indias, Ceylon, and Burma, might be the answer.

Tentative soundings were made to discover the reactions of the party leaders to these alternative schemes. Gandhi seemed to be at a loss: he envisaged that the divisions would lead to a bloodbath, and he was doubtful how far the Congress would observe non-violence. Jinnah reiterated the six provinces' demand: if there was to be a compromise, then let the Mission enunciate this. He would not make premature concessions which might encourage the Congress to demand further areas from the League's Pakistan. The obduracy of Jinnah began to have an adverse effect. Cripps, at any rate, felt that it was essential to have the support of one of the parties, and if Jinnah rejected all attempts to meet his position at least half-way, then a bid must be made to secure the co-operation of Congress. To this, Alexander replied that the British public would not tolerate abandoning the Muslims: especially if this meant excluding them from the Commonwealth. An announcement on Palestine was imminent, and this was likely to make concessions to the Jewish claims. Supposing there was an outburst of Islamic feeling in the Middle East? Britain could not expect to ignore with impunity the whole Muslim world.

The three-tier solution

Cripps proceeded to refine his first proposal, postulating three tiers of political control, the provincial, the regional, and the central. It was an ingenious device which should enable power to flow at its natural level. If the national forces proved strongest, then the centre would develop. If regional or religious separatism continued to be dominant, then this scheme provided for separate development between 'Pakistan' and 'Hindustan', encapsulated within a tenuous Indian unity. The scheme also allowed for a situation such as had developed in the NWFP where the Red Shirts had set up a provincial government beyond the 'Pakistan' stronghold of Punjab: Congress was exhibiting an understandable but dangerous solicitude for this outpost of its empire. Wavell emphasized that if the Mission was going to commit itself to the three-tier plan, then this must be accompanied by a thoroughgoing rejection of Pakistan. The difficulties and dangers of partition must be exposed, so that the whole Pakistan concept was disposed of, leaving the Cabinet Mission scheme holding the field. If the scheme was just and equitable, and put through with firmness, it would be accepted.

At first, it seemed that this assessment of the reactions of the parties would be fulfilled. Confronted with the alternatives of a three-tier confederation, conceding a maximum of autonomy for the six 'Pakistan' provinces, or a minimum Pakistan, Jinnah agreed to consider the former scheme. Soon afterwards Cripps reported that the

Congress President, Abul Kalam Azad, had asked him for an interview and spontaneously volunteered the opinion that he could get the Congress Working Committee to agree to negotiate with the League on the basis of an all-India Union confined to foreign affairs, defence, and communications, with a legislature which would meet in two parts to deal with optional subjects. If Jinnah would agree to negotiate on this basis, he was confident that he could get his committee to agree to nominate four representatives to have discussions with the League and the Mission on this formula.

In his desire to find a solution based upon Indian unity, while believing that only by confronting the party leaders with harsh alternatives would they face reality, Cripps may have exaggerated the extent to which Azad was ready to commit himself and his colleagues. But this seemed to be the first real break-through, and the Mission shelved their plan to publish the scheme *ex cathedra* and hastened to convene a conference to carry it through by agreement.

From this time, Azad emerged as the principal Congress spokesman, and Gandhi was relegated to an occasional appearance and frequent utterances 'off stage'. Gandhi's role thus far had been too equivocal and nebulous to constitute a contribution to the negotiations. At one moment he spoke in apocalyptic tones, as the detached observer, the oracle; then he would unexpectedly speak as one wholly *engagé* in the Congress cause. There was no formal change; but henceforward Gandhi was treated by the Mission as a kind of court of final appeal in the formulation of Congress policy: he was not consulted in the day-by-day discussions. The other Congress leaders concurred in this proceeding being themselves, embarrassed by Gandhi's tendency to raise difficulties at this time.

Grouping: the attempted compromise

In his invitations to the Congress and League to join in a conference at Simla, the Secretary of State indicated that the detailed settlement would be based upon certain fundamental principles.[3] The constitution would provide for a Union government dealing with foreign affairs, defence, and communications. There would be two groups of provinces—the predominantly Hindu, and predominantly Muslim provinces—'dealing with all other subjects which the provinces in the respective groups desire to be dealt with in common. The Provincial Governments will deal with all other subjects and will have all the residuary Sovereign rights.' This approach envisaged a situation like that of the American states under the original articles of confederation, with the provinces providing the units to make the ultimate choice as to how much sovereign power (apart from the subjects given to the centre) would be assigned to the groups.

In their replies, both Azad for the Congress and Jinnah for the League made considerable reservations—the one for a united India, the other for Pakistan—but both accepted the invitation. To underline its national character, the Congress nominated Jawaharlal Nehru, Vallabhbhai Patel, Azad, and Abdul Ghaffar Khan, premier of the NWFP.

The Mission occupied the time before the conference began by further revising the draft scheme.[4] They began to look ahead to the implications of this balance of

[3] *Correspondence and Documents connected with the Conference between the Cabinet Mission and His Excellency the Viceroy and Representatives of the Congress and the Muslim League, May 1946.* Cmd. 6829 (covers period 27 April–12 May).

[4] At the time, this was invariably called the Cabinet Mission Plan. Later, when Lord Mountbatten formulated his constitutional proposals these were also called the Plan. In order to distinguish between the two, the Cabinet Mission Plan is called the 'Scheme' in this book, while Mountbatten's Plan is called the 'Deal'. No pejorative distinction is intended.

powers, and to consider questions such as whether the two 'federations' (as they were treated) would have their own flags and their own, limited, security forces.

One substantial change in the scheme was made as the result of a draft submitted by Sir B. N. Rau, the Constitutional Adviser, and V. P. Menon, Reforms Commissioner. They suggested that instead of the 'Hindustan' and 'Pakistan' grouping of provinces there should be three groups. The two wings of 'Pakistan' should be listed separately as Groups B and C. In this way, it was argued, the emphasis upon a religious division would be diminished, and the grouping would appear partly as an administrative measure—the last of the many measures of devolution. Also, Bengal and Assam, as having only a marginal Muslim majority, might emerge in a mediating role between the Muslim north-west and the Hindu heartland. This argument was accepted, and the 'Pakistan' aspect of the scheme became implicit rather than explicit. A further vexed question upon which Rau and Menon tendered advice was that of the status of the Cabinet Mission scheme: should it be presented as an award—i.e. with mandatory authority—like the Communal Award of 1931, or should it be advanced as a proposal which the party leaders would be required to implement for themselves? It was decided to adopt the latter course; to work to secure agreement upon the scheme, but leaving the final decision on acceptance or rejection to the representatives of the peoples of India. The Mission cabled the terms of their scheme to London, in advance of the Simla meeting, in case it should become necessary to release it in its existing form if no agreement emerged from the Congress–League dialogue. The scheme fell into two parts: a lengthy preliminary examination of various versions of Pakistan, and the rejection of the division of India into two separate sovereign states, and secondly, an enunciation

of the three-tier scheme, with the three groups or sections
A (Madras, Bombay, UP, Bihar, Central Provinces
Orissa), B (Punjab, North-West Frontier, and Sind), and
C (Bengal and Assam).

Second Simla conference

In preparing for the Simla conference, it was again
decided that the Mission would take the line that their
role was that of honest broker, without any special desire
to press one scheme or another. But an attempt was made
to steer the proceedings toward the three-tier solution by
setting out an agenda in which the conference would begin
by considering the position of the provinces and their
grouping, followed by a review of the nature of the Union
government, finishing with the actual machinery for
drafting the constitution at the different levels.

The second Simla conference opened on 5 May, and
immediately the carefully-drawn agenda was tossed aside.
The Congress attempted to begin by reinforcing the powers
of the central government. The League replied by trying
to divest the centre of any corporate status, reducing it to
a meeting-point between the groups. Azad followed up
this preliminary encounter by tendering a letter to
Pethick-Lawrence which made it clear that Congress
would not accept the grouping principle as a prior
condition. Indeed, he endeavoured to revive the approach
of the Lahore 'declaration of independence' of 1929,
insisting that the purpose of their meeting was to agree
upon independence and the setting up of a Constituent
Assembly, leaving all the details of constitution-making
to the Assembly which (Azad specified) would not be
bound by prior commitments entered into with the
British or others. The discussion on 6 May followed these
propositions. Nehru brushed aside the question of group-

.ng, though he acknowledged that if any province declined
to enter the Constituent Assembly (and no attempt was
made to deny this right) then the Assembly should proceed without it. If this meant that the projected all-India
union had to be diminished, then the Congress was ready
to accept this loss. Attempts to remind the Congress
leaders that the fate of India was in the balance did not
affect their attitude. It was obvious that the conference
was drifting, so Pethick-Lawrence and his colleagues
suggested a recess on 8 May, and drafted a memorandum
of 'Suggested Points for Agreement between the representatives of the Congress and the Muslim League'.

Grouping diluted

As was to be common practice in the following months,
the refusal of the Congress leaders to compromise had the
effect of inducing the British to shift their position in order
to try, desperately, to cling to the shreds of agreement
already concluded. The 'Points of Agreement' (which
were, of course, features, some old, some new, which the
Cabinet Mission and Viceroy thought might be accepted
in some form) began by extending a little the scope of the
centre. It went on to reiterate that 'All the remaining
powers shall vest in the provinces'. This concern with the
'States' Rights' aspect of the provinces was being emphasized by the British and the Congress for entirely
opposed reasons. The British inferred that this endowed
the provinces with the right to hive off into groups. The
Congress believed that the Congress loyalties of the provincial governments of Assam and the North-West
Frontier would put a stop to any move to form such
groups. The third and fourth propositions in the 'Points
of Agreement' stated that 'Groups of provinces *may* be
formed and such groups *may* determine the Provincial

subjects which they desire to take in common. The groups
may set up their own Executives and Legislatures.'[5] This
interpretation clearly moved away from the original
'fundamental principles' which had said 'There *will* be
two groups of Provinces'. This was a long step towards the
Congress insistence on the optional, hypothetical role of
the groups. In order to give something back to the League,
a new proposal was inserted to make it possible for any
province to 'call for a reconsideration of the terms of the
constitution' after ten years. Further, the 'Points of
Agreement' went on to plunge even more into unexplored
territory by sketching out the procedure for constitution-
making, which would provide for three separate sections—
the Hindu- and Muslim-majority provinces, and the
princely states respectively; the first two would meet to
draft provincial and ('if they wish') group constitutions:
subsequently it would be open to any province to opt out
of its group, to join another group, or to stay outside any
group.

Jinnah protests

Clearly, these proposals invited protest from the Muslim
League: and Jinnah promptly tendered a letter of dissent,
claiming that no useful purpose would be served by discussing them. However, the bid to secure the adherence of
Congress was equally unsuccessful. A letter from Azad the
next day set out to demolish the proposals in detail, and
to emphasize that constitution-making was the task of a
Constituent Assembly representative of the Indian peoples.
Whatever element of mandatory grouping remained was
repudiated. On a note of bombast Azad demanded: 'Why
should the Frontier Province, which is clearly a Congress
Province, be compelled to join any group hostile to the

[5] Italics added.

Congress?' The sole indication of any awareness that there were differences of opinion between the leaders of India came at the end, in a suggestion that matters in dispute between Congress and League should be referred to 'an independent tribunal'.

This last point led to a suggestion by Nehru that both sides should sit together with an umpire to discuss points at issue, and in case of disagreement should accept the umpire's decision as final. Jinnah was not prepared to fling into the arena those points which he regarded as fundamental. There was an exchange of notes—from Nehru, bland, from Jinnah, icy—and then the proposal collapsed. Was Nehru following Gandhi's course of trying by the gesture of surrendering all claims to win back his opponent's confidence? Or was this (as later events were to suggest) a device for taking the case to a supreme judicial tribunal where there would be infinite possibilities of employing legal techniques on appeal? As the 'umpire' proposal was never fully developed, there can be no answer. Nothing remained but to bring the conference to a close. A last memorandum submitted by Jinnah, suggesting a formula which would concede almost the full Pakistan demand, and a counter-proposal by the Congress designed to bring an all-India Constituent Assembly into being cannot be regarded as anything but propaganda gestures. Jinnah was so irritated by the way the conference had been manoeuvred that he insisted on publication of all the correspondence. This was now to become common form, and it is difficult to feel from this time forward that any letter was drafted by the Viceroy or the Mission to a political leader, or vice versa, except with an eye to eventual publication. As there were no longer any truly confidential communications between the three sides, the prospect of any genuine concession being made became negligible.

While the conference proceeded, from 5 to 11 May, the

British government was considering the draft Cabinet
Mission scheme. This received a not over-enthusiastic
endorsement. So much seemed to be lacking exact
definition, especially with regard to the groups. An ingenious suggestion was made that if a province insisted on
entering another group it might upset the communal
balance (as if Bihar were to link up with Bengal and
Assam). Fortunately, amid their many trials, the Cabinet
Mission were not required to deal with this contingency.
Final revisions for the forthcoming statement were made
after the Simla conference had ended. The vexed question
of the character of the groups, optional or mandatory, was
covered by the phrase: 'Provinces should be free to form
groups with executives and legislatures'. The Mission
withstood final suggestions from Whitehall on further
amendments and qualifications. Their general line was to
say the least that would cover future developments, in the
belief that any apparent attempt to propel the leaders of
the new India in a specified direction would only lead
them to move in an opposite direction. The experience of
seven weeks of unceasing argument, culminating in the
frustrations of the Simla conference, had left their mark
upon the Mission.

The Scheme announced

The 'Statement by the Cabinet Delegation and His
Excellency the Viceroy' issued on 16 May 1946 was in
essence the three-tier plan which had already been rejected by Congress and the League.[6] The Mission cannot
have expected an enthusiastic reception. The only hope
was that somehow public opinion would be manifested
in such a way as to influence the high commands of the

[6] *India (Cabinet Mission): Statement by the Cabinet Delegation and His Excellency
the Viceroy, 16th May 1946.* Cmd. 6821.

two contesting parties. This was a slender hope, when recent events had demonstrated what a tight system of discipline prevailed within the inner core of leadership in both parties.

The Cabinet Mission's proposals fell into two main parts: an outline of the constitutional framework which they anticipated, and a firm arrangement for constitution-making machinery.

The framework was to be a Union of India, responsible for foreign affairs, defence, and communications, with an executive and a legislature 'constituted from British Indian and States representatives'. This represented a somewhat stronger centre than had once been contemplated. All other subjects were vested in the provinces—and the states and 'provinces should be free to form groups'. The provision for 'reconsidering' the terms of the constitution after ten years followed.

In setting up a Constituent Assembly, the Mission abandoned the various developments from the Lucknow Pact onwards whereby the Muslims had secured a voice in public affairs in excess of their actual numbers in the population. Having obtained one-third of the seats in the Dyarchy central assembly, the Muslims had been moving to the point where they might have obtained parity with Hindus in a Union legislature. But the formula for setting up a Constituent Assembly went back to the realities of the Census figures. The various provincial legislatures were to elect the members of the Constituent Assembly by pro-portional representation on a basis of one member for every million of population covered. This gave the Muslim community 78 representatives out of a total of 292 for British India. The Sikhs were to return four represen-tatives. The remainder, the 'General' members, might be expected to consist mainly of Congress nominees.

If the Muslims were thus 'cut down to size', their rights

were safeguarded by the procedure laid down for the Assembly. After a preliminary meeting, the members would divide up into sections (the A, B, and C groups) which would settle the provincial constitutions for each section, deciding also whether any group constitution should be formed. As soon as the constitutional arrangements were finalized, a province might opt out of the group in which it was placed; but only after a fresh election had been held under the new constitution.

The statement went on to indicate that as an interim measure the Viceroy would re-form his Executive Council to obtain the support of the major political parties. There were urgent practical problems to be tackled, including a grave danger of famine. The statement closed with a grim note of warning:

We ask you to consider the alternative to acceptance of these proposals. . . . In our view there is small hope of peaceful settlement by agreement of the Indian parties alone. The alternative would therefore be a grave danger of violence, chaos, and even civil war. . . . It is certain that it would be a terrible disaster for many millions of men, women and children.

4

The Scheme Rejected, and Accepted
(May-June 1946)

ON the day that the Cabinet Mission scheme was published, Wavell met Azad and Nehru and emphasized that this was the last chance of securing a unified India. There was no immediate response from either Congress or the League, and the Viceroy and ministers made an interim attempt to analyse the strategy of the party leaders. Wavell believed that the objective of the Congress was to seize power at the centre. If they could prolong the process of arguing about the constitution until British troops had left the country, and could gain control over the police and the Indian army, then they could deal with the Muslims and the Princes as they wished. The only way to persuade the Congress leaders that they would not succeed would be to make it crystal clear that British rule would remain until an agreed constitution had been concluded. Even Cripps was prepared to agree that one leading element in Congress planned to take this course.

The letters which followed from Gandhi and Azad seemed to corroborate this analysis. Gandhi emphasized that the scheme was a recommendation, and it was therefore left to provinces like Assam and the NWFP to abstain from adhering to the sections to which they were assigned. British troops must go, or independence would be meaningless. Azad insisted that the Constituent Assembly was a sovereign body, and it was therefore open to the

Assembly to vary in any way it liked the recommendations and procedure suggested by the Cabinet Mission. He also called for the withdrawal of British troops: 'India should be considered to be independent in fact from the moment that the National Provisional Government is established.'

These letters caused the Mission to stiffen their attitude. Cripps now succumbed to one of his many bouts of illness, but he concurred in insisting that Azad's claim to sovereign status for the Constituent Assembly must be rejected. Pethick-Lawrence raised the question of future policy if Congress now launched another mass campaign on Quit India lines. The alternatives open to the British were (in theory at any rate) three: repression, immediate withdrawal, or a phased withdrawal. The Viceroy's immediate reaction was to identify the different faces of the Congress. There were the ministries, anxious to remain in office; there was Jayaprakash Narayan, then kept firmly in the background, but a potent focus for a campaign of violence; there was the INA, somewhat discredited, but still dangerous; and there was Gandhi, who might turn difficult. Trouble must be expected in the UP and Bihar, the arena of the 1942 disturbances. The Viceroy agreed to prepare a detailed appreciation of the situation on the lines of his Middle East 'worst possible case' analyses.

Grouping upheld by the Mission

On 22 May the Viceroy and ministers replied to Azad insisting that 'the scheme stands as a whole and can only succeed if it is accepted and worked in a spirit of compromise and co-operation'. Grouping was said to be an essential feature of the scheme, only to be modified by agreement between the two parties. Finally, Congress was reminded that independence would follow, not precede, the constitution-making. The response of the Congress was to issue a resolution on the 24th which defined their objective as a strong though limited central authority, with full autonomy for the provinces. On grouping, the resolution concluded: 'The Committee read paragraph 15 [of the Cabinet Mission Statement] to mean that, in the first instance, the respective provinces will make their choice whether or not to belong to the section in which they are placed.' A statement was promptly issued indicating that the Congress interpretation 'does not accord with the Delegation's intentions'. It went on: 'The right to opt out of the groups after the constitution making has been completed will be exercised by the people themselves.'[1]

This attempt to refer the decision on the groups from the party chiefs to the people did not deflect the Congress high command. On the same day Azad approached Wavell 'for a formal understanding by which the Congress Working Committee may be assured that the interim government would in practice function like a Dominion Cabinet': this would introduce the convention that the government depended for its authority on the confidence of the Constituent Assembly. Wavell rejected this attempt to induce him to sign away his powers, but in his letter of 30 May he tried to break free from the current atmosphere of suspicion and bargaining by declaring:

I am quite clear that the spirit in which the government is worked will be of much greater importance than any formal document and guarantee. . . . I have no doubt that if you are prepared to trust me, we shall be able to co-operate in a manner which will give India a sense of freedom from external control and will prepare for complete freedom as soon as the new constitution is made.

Such an emphasis upon trust and mutual confidence might have been expected to evoke an ardent response

[1] *India (Cabinet Mission): Statement by the Mission dated 25th May in reply to pronouncements by the Indian Parties . . . May 1946.* Cmd. 6835 (includes statements by League of 22 May, and Congress, 24 May).

from Gandhi in better days. But during the current period of negotiations, and during the subsequent months, Gandhi seems to have adopted an attitude quite different from his characteristic magnanimity, opposing any concessions and stiffening the attitude of his colleagues whenever they appeared disposed to compromise. Could it be that Gandhi recalled his other major encounters with Smuts and Halifax when he had responded to appeals to show trust, and in the outcome had been offered something a good deal less than might have been obtained by obduracy? Whatever the reason, the absence of conciliation and compromise during the next two months was to prove fatal to the last chance of resolving the differences between Congress and League.

Wavell's alternatives

In reply to Pethick-Lawrence's questions, Wavell now submitted a long memorandum on the alternatives which might be expected, and measures which might be taken. The Viceroy had to keep in mind the lessons which had been so wearily learned. There was little hope of co-operation between Congress and League, so long as Jinnah's suspicions of Gandhi and others were not assuaged. The Sikhs were becoming restless. The great mass of the people were still quite reconciled to British rule, but they might easily be stirred into violence. Trouble might come at any time and without any prior warning, as so often in the past. The Viceroy had to see through the task of giving India self-government, while at the same time maintaining his normal responsibilities for law and order. It was not practical politics to think of replying to an all-out Congress outbreak by rigorous repression, unless Britain were prepared to stay in India for a decade or more. GHQ had already presented the Viceroy with a military plan for holding the great ports in order to carry out an orderly withdrawal. What, then, were the practical applications of these factors to the three alternatives posed by the Secretary of State?

Wavell indicated that he would be prepared to see through a long-term operation ('repression') though it was unlikely that the British government and people would want this. He was not prepared to be responsible for unconditional and immediate withdrawal ('scuttle'). Was there, then, a middle course between repression and scuttle? The provision in the 1942 Cripps offer for 'opting out' seemed to provide an alternative. The Hindu-majority provinces could be transferred to 'Hindu' rule. The Muslim-majority provinces would continue under British rule until such time as their leaders had worked out their own constitution.

There were obvious dangers and difficulties in such a course. The Indian army would have to be divided. The large minorities of Hindus and Sikhs in the Muslim-majority provinces would be a British responsibility. The arrangement must not become permanent, leading to another 'Northern Ireland'. But the main advantage of the plan was that it kept the options open. Quite probably, such a course would lead to the emergence of Pakistan; but it would demonstrate to the Congress that unless they were prepared to negotiate and compromise, this was the inevitable conclusion to the conflict. Given a new spirit of compromise, it would be possible to bring about reunion and a Union of India on the best terms possible. That would be the moment for the British to withdraw. Meanwhile, the Congress would be deprived of its trump card (as contemporary British thinking saw it): the ability to mount a revolt in UP and Bihar by which to threaten British authority. Relieved of this threat, the British administration could concentrate on the problems of the north-west and eastern India.

Considering the immediate problem of forming an interim government, Wavell had to face three possibilities. If Congress and the League agreed to join, all should be well. It was difficult to imagine a contingency in which Congress stayed out and the League formed a government, as Jinnah could not exercise authority in the Hindu provinces. The greatest problem could arise if Congress agreed to come in while the League stood out. This could lead to grave disorders in Punjab and Bengal. In case of disagreement, one temporary solution might be for a 'Hindustan' government to be created for the Congress provinces and a 'Pakistan' government for the Muslim-majority provinces, with a purely official government at the centre. Even if the best happened, and a coalition government, together with a Constituent Assembly came into being, still every attempt to sap British authority must be expected from the Congress side.

As May passed into June there was no sign of the political leaders coming forward to accept the Cabinet Mission scheme on any kind of basis of agreement. The Viceroy and the ministers (Cripps was still confined to hospital) therefore refined their proposals for alternative courses of action. An alternative not hitherto considered was to refer the whole problem to the United Nations; but experience of the UN treatment of the Palestine issue discouraged this solution. At last the Viceroy and his colleagues felt the time had arrived to place their analysis of the situation and probable developments before the Cabinet in order to obtain a directive for action in case of breakdown. It seemed possible that a crisis might arise within a few days. The three alternatives open to Britain —repression, scuttle, and withdrawal into the north-west and the east—were canvassed. The weight of opinion lay with the scheme for partial transfer of power and consolidation in the Muslim-majority provinces, though Cripps from his sickbed dissented and advocated a variation on 'scuttle', whereby Britain would declare an intention to withdraw from India by a stipulated date. By this means it might be possible to achieve the result hoped from the partial transfer scheme: a realization among the Indian leaders that Britain was in earnest, so that they would abandon their differences.

In London the Cabinet was immune from the sense of desperation and the growing tensions which pressed upon the Viceroy and the Mission. The Prime Minister pointed out the obvious possibility that the partial transfer scheme might have the effect of giving to Jinnah the Pakistan which had so far been resisted. Britain must continue to discharge its responsibilities in India until the Indian leaders had agreed upon a basis to accept the British offer of independence. If a Congress revolt developed it might be necessary to modify this policy, but the Cabinet was not convinced that such a revolt was imminent.

Overtures for an interim government

Having formulated two entirely different approaches to independence, and having seen the one rejected by Congress, and the other rejected by the British government, the Viceroy and the Mission returned to the task of trying to persuade Congress and League to take part in an interim government. Jinnah put it to Wavell that if the League accepted the Cabinet plan and Congress subsequently rejected it, he wanted an assurance that the League would be brought into an interim government. After consulting his colleagues, Wavell gave this assurance on 4 June: 'We shall go ahead with the plan laid down in the statement, so far as circumstances permit, if either party accepts: but we hope that both will accept.' Following this assurance, on 6 June the Council of the League accepted the plan, though insisting that 'the attainment of the goal of a complete sovereign Pakistan still remains the unalterable objective of the Muslims of India'. The League inevitably laid stress upon the grouping formula and on the right of provinces to secede from the Indian Union.

On 10 June the Viceroy and the ministers met Azad and Nehru in an attempt to persuade them to participate in an interim government. As a basis for negotiation, a formula of 5:5:2 was suggested, with equal representation ('parity') between Congress and the League, and with two members drawn from the minorities, one of whom might be a Congress ally. Nehru was in his most intransigent mood. He dismissed the League and its leaders as men without principles or policies. He said quite frankly that the Congress would work for a strong centre, and to break up the groups: and the Congress would succeed. Pethick-Lawrence tried to get across the idea that a coalition must work together, transcending the sentiment of a majority and a minority. Alexander tried to indicate the need for Congress to make concessions, to meet the point of view of others; reminding Nehru that Jinnah had been required to swallow a bitter pill in the rejection of Pakistan by the Cabinet Mission scheme. Unless they tried to work together, it would prove impossible to assimilate the Muslims into an Indian nation. None of this had any effect upon Nehru's attitude. Next day the Viceroy met Gandhi, who was in one of his Olympian moods. He waved aside mundane questions, such as the numerical proportions of the parties, insisting that the coalition must be a homogeneous team. He advised the Viceroy to bring Nehru and Jinnah together, and not permit them to depart until they had agreed upon a government. However, though Wavell followed up this suggestion, the joint meeting could not be arranged.

By mid-June, Wavell and his colleagues had come to

feel that further delay must inevitably lead to a deterioration in the situation. A panel of names was therefore transmitted to London for the King's approval, in case it was thought desirable to designate the personnel of an interim government *ex cathedra*.

An interim government announced

On 14 June the Viceroy received two letters from Azad. The Congress President made a point of thanking Wavell for the friendly tone of his letter of 30 May, but went on to object to certain features of representation in the Constituent Assembly, and also opposed the principle of parity as between Congress and League membership in the interim government. Next day, Wavell replied, saying that he deduced from Azad's reservations that the attempt to negotiate an agreement between the two major parties on the composition of the interim government had failed. When the ministers met the Viceroy next day, Cripps reported that Patel was said to be insisting that the interim government must contain 15 members: 5 Muslim, 5 Congress, and 5 from the minorities, who might include Congress allies. The Secretary of State was moved to say that what troubled him was whether Congress intended to accept any long-term settlement, or would there always be additional conditions? There was some difference of opinion on whether Jinnah should be invited to form an interim government: Cripps held that he should be asked. However, it was decided to issue a statement, naming a new government. This statement of 16 June briefly mentioned the difficulties which had arisen in trying to obtain agreement. It went on to state that the Viceroy was issuing invitations to fourteen persons. These were 6 Congress members (Nehru, Krishna Mahtab of Orissa, Rajagopalachari, Rajendra Prasad, Patel, Jagjivan Ram,

President of the All-India Depressed Class League), 5 League members (Jinnah, Liaqat Ali Khan, Mohammad Ismail Khan, Nazimuddin, Abdur Rab Nishtar), and Baldev Singh (Sikh), Sir N. P. Engineer (Parsi), Federal Advocate General, and John Matthai (Christian). This represented a distribution of power which gave Congress an edge over the League, but which left no party in a position to dominate the government.

Paragraph 8 of the statement was as follows:

> In the event of the two major parties or either of them proving unwilling to join in setting up a Coalition Government on the above lines, it is the intention of the Viceroy to proceed with the formation of an Interim Government which will be as representative as possible of those willing to accept the Statement of May 16th.[2]

This paragraph was in line with Wavell's assurance to Jinnah, and was both an inducement and a warning. The statement went on to signify that the Governors had been directed to put into motion the machinery for electing the members of the Constituent Assembly. Finally, there was yet another appeal to the contending parties for partnership.

Once again, as in the case of their constitutional scheme, the Viceroy and his colleagues began by making a confidential offer to Congress and the League, and when that failed attempted to challenge them by publicly issuing the same proposals. Yet again, the response from both sides was to embark on a series of bargaining encounters, in order to win a little or a lot more than the statement offered. On 17 June it was reported that Patel was violently opposed to Congress acceptance of the offer, while Gandhi was favourably inclined. Yet when the Congress Working Committee met on the 19th and

[2] *India (Cabinet Mission): Correspondence with the Congress Party and the Muslim League, 20th May–29th June, 1946,* Cmd. 6861.

favoured acceptance if the name of S. C. Bose was sub-
stituted for that of Mahtab (a change acceptable to the
Viceroy), Gandhi was pressing Azad to take a place on
the Council: although Jinnah's refusal to acknowledge the
Nationalist Muslims was one of the chief stumbling-
blocks. Meantime, Jinnah was entering into discussions on
the *modus operandi* of the new government, having already
accepted the Cabinet Mission scheme, as required in the
16 June statement. The Viceroy and his colleagues devoted much time to the question of the terms on which the
League should enter the government assuming that the
Congress rejected the terms. Should Jinnah be asked to
nominate a panel of names, acting as *de facto* Prime
Minister? Or should the Viceroy form the government,
making up the Hindu quota from the liberals and non-
party public men? Supposing that Jinnah declined to
accept this second procedure? Would it then be incumbent
on Wavell to make another approach to the Congress to
form a government? There was a danger in all this that
Jinnah might feel that the British had not kept faith with
him when he had taken the lead in adjusting his claims to
the offers of 16 May and 16 June.

Congress responses

A note of almost frantic urgency had entered into the
discussions. The Mission had been in India almost three
months; Cripps was ill, and Pethick-Lawrence almost
exhausted, while Alexander was scarcely able to contain
his irritation at the treatment they had received from the
Congress. It was high time they went: and the Secretary
of State announced that they must leave within a few days.[3]

[3] On 22 June Pethick-Lawrence wrote to his wife. 'The political baro-
meter has gone so up and down that I really don't know from day to day
what the final result will be. . . . People start coming to interview me at
7 a.m. and the last doesn't leave much before midnight. And nothing whatever comes of it! And the heat is stifling' (Brittain, pp. 173-4).

On 23 June Pethick-Lawrence had a meeting with Patel which developed on unexpected lines. Patel said that the Congress had decided against entry into the government because they had given way to the Muslim League on every point so far. Pethick-Lawrence retorted that the League had made the concession of accepting the long-term scheme which the Congress had not done. Patel replied that the Congress had certainly accepted the statement of 16 May and added that they were going to work the long-term plan in any case, regardless of the interim government controversy. Pethick-Lawrence replied somewhat tartly that it was news to him that Congress had accepted the scheme.

Next day the Viceroy and the ministers considered whether they should meet the Congress leaders again. Patel was now said to be in favour of the scheme without reservation. A meeting had been arranged with Gandhi and Patel for the same evening, but Alexander objected that they ought to keep Jinnah informed, as he had played straight whereas the behaviour of the Congress was unpredictable. It was clearly necessary to decide what to say to Jinnah if the Congress should accept the scheme, while still making reservations. By accepting the scheme, the Congress would become eligible to join the government, even though they had objected to the distribution of membership previously propounded. As against this, there was paragraph 8 of the 16 June statement, indicating that the Viceroy would go ahead with an interim government if one of the major parties declined to participate. One, or both, of the parties was going to feel aggrieved at whatever action was taken. Alexander suggested that a government of officials could be reconstituted, pending agreement between the parties on participation. Wavell agreed, although he felt that his senior officials were beginning to flag, and the official government ought to be of short duration.[4]

When the Viceroy and his colleagues met Gandhi and Patel the same evening, Wavell attempted once again to establish that the decision on grouping would be taken by a majority vote within the sections and that provinces could not opt out initially of their own volition. Gandhi dissented, adding that his view of the document was upheld by eminent lawyers. The Cabinet Mission were the lawgivers, and could not interpret their own law. It must be for the Federal Court to give a judicial interpretation of its meaning. Gandhi went on to point out that the Constituent Assembly had no statutory existence: because the Mission had created a statement which had no legal existence. Therefore Congress insisted that independence must mean independence *now*. Otherwise, there could be a change of government in Britain and the policy of the British government might change.

All this was too much for Pethick-Lawrence who interrupted to say that it was not the practice of British governments to repudiate pledges entered into by their predecessors. As for giving the Constituent Assembly statutory authority, Mr Gandhi would be the first to object if the Mission said that the formation of the Constituent

[4] One of the factors weighing heavily with Wavell, and later with Mountbatten, was a conviction that the British administrators in India had reached the end of their tether and could not be called upon for any long-term course of action. In this, the Viceroys seem to have been unduly influenced by the performance of a few very senior officials in New Delhi. The present author was then working as a junior civilian in the UP, and there was no sign of ICS colleagues having shot their bolt. They were worried about the uncertainty: particularly over the absence of any agreement about their pension rights. But subsequently many of these British ICS men in their middle or late 40s went on to carve out distinguished second careers in the Foreign Service and elsewhere, while the Hindu and Muslim ICS men were to carry India and Pakistan on their shoulders for nearly twenty years. Perhaps if Wavell had established a greater degree of contact with his Governors and other senior administrators he would have felt that he could call upon the provincial and district administration for reserves of effort, and this might have strengthened his hand.

Assembly must wait for an enabling Bill to be passed through parliament. The encounter seemed to demonstrate that the Congress and the British leaders were living in separate, enclosed worlds. The British had no real understanding of the outlook of the Congress leadership, and the latter were unable to appreciate either that they were actually on the threshold of independence or that the realities of politics in the sub-continent made some distribution of power inevitable.

The Scheme accepted, the interim government postponed

The 25th of June brought a letter from Azad, almost at the end of his period of office as Congress President. He wrote:

> With regard to the proposals made in the statement of 16th May 1946 . . . the Working Committee of the Congress passed a resolution on the 24th May 1946, and conversations and correspondence have taken place. . . . In these we have pointed out what in our opinion were the defects of the proposals. We also gave our interpretation of some of the provisions of the statement. While adhering to our views, we accept your proposals and are prepared to work them with a view to achieve our objective. We would add, however, that the successful working of the Constituent Assembly will largely depend on the formation of a satisfactory Provisional Government.[5]

The Viceroy and the ministers met at noon to consider this letter. It was agreed that, although cleverly worded, this must be regarded as an acceptance of the long-term proposals. There were no illusions left. The ministers were just as aware as the Viceroy that this had settled nothing: all the difficulties which had been paraded dur-

[5] Cmd. 6861.

ing the forty days after publication of their scheme remained to cause trouble at any time. Wavell was frankly hostile: an acceptance by the Congress which they meant to break was worse than a refusal. But the Cabinet Mission were tired, and desperately anxious to return home. This was a conclusion of a sort, and they accepted it. There was general agreement that Azad's letter with its rejection of the formula proposed on 16 June put paid to any immediate attempt to form an interim government.

And so Jinnah had to be told that despite his acceptance of both the 16 May and 16 June statements, his party would not now be entering an interim government. Naturally the encounter with Jinnah was stormy. Pethick-Lawrence pointed out that both the League and the Congress had put their own gloss upon the scheme. Jinnah replied that the Congress reservation was different in kind: it would insist that the Constituent Assembly's first item of business was to decide whether provinces should opt out of their group at the outset. Doubtless Jinnah was correct in his diagnosis: but it was somewhat disingenuous to pass over the fact that the Muslim League had announced that it was only entering the scheme in order to work out its objective, Pakistan. However, there was little appeal to reason on this occasion.

The 26th of June saw the last encounters between the Cabinet Mission and the party leaders. A meeting with Azad, Nehru, and Patel was utilized to emphasize that the essence of the 16 May scheme was the grouping formula. Azad plainly indicated that the Congress would try to persuade the Constituent Assembly against following this course. When Pethick-Lawrence reiterated that the section meetings must go ahead, with the right to opt out being reserved for the period after the constitution had been framed, Nehru oracularly replied that they might possibly get over these obstacles or they might not.

Already Nehru saw himself in an almost predestined role; the murmurings of these Englishmen made no impression. The meeting with Jinnah was conducted by Alexander alone, on behalf of his colleagues. The homely Baptist lay-preacher had established an unexpected empathy with the immaculate, withdrawn barrister. But on this occasion he could do little to mollify the Muslim League chief, who was convinced that he had been ditched in order to avoid severing relations with the Congress.

On 26 June an announcement appeared: 'It is proposed that further negotiations [on the formation of the interim government] should be adjourned for a short interval during the time while the elections for the Constituent Assembly will be taking place.' An official caretaker regime was to be installed.

The last meeting between the Viceroy, the Secretary of State, Cripps, and Alexander took place on 28 June. It was agreed to publish the whole correspondence with Congress and the League.[6] Next day the Mission departed, leaving Wavell to soldier on, to find solutions to the textual conundrums created by Cripps in his frenetic attempts to devise acceptable formulae; to bring into some sort of communication the elusive Congress and League. The Mission had not achieved a fraction of what they expected to accomplish at the start. But they had made a beginning. They had demonstrated that the British government was in earnest. They had demonstrated that the British leaders were human beings, ready to respond to any gesture of humanity made by the Indian leaders. And they had demonstrated to the leaders of both the major parties that there was no Open Sesame to independence.

[6] *India (Cabinet Mission): Papers relating to (a) the Sikhs, (b) the Indian States and (c) the European Community, May–June 1946*, Cmd. 6862.

Perhaps, without directly intending this, the Mission had helped to keep India quiet during the months April–July, often the most riot-torn period of the year. Because political India had its attention focused upon the activities of the Mission, there were no serious disturbances. In February there had been the Indian navy revolt in Bombay and a serious communal riot in Calcutta. During the next three months India had waited: but the latent tensions could not be suppressed much longer.

5

The Withering of the Scheme
(July-December 1946)

THE Cabinet Mission had seen their first task as securing the agreement of Congress to a scheme which would give the Muslims a recognized political position, yet would preserve the essential unity of the sub-continent. In order to gain the goodwill of Congress and to allay its suspicions of British intentions, they had, whether consciously or not, to modify both the short-term and long-term arrangements in ways to appease the major party. The League had seen its demand for Pakistan categorically rejected, and had sensed that the political tide was not flowing its way: it had therefore shown a spirit of accommodation, as the best means of maintaining its standing as an organization having 'parity' (or near-parity) with Congress. However, it was now becoming clear that the British policy of appeasement, far from making the Congress more co-operative, was increasing its sense of manifest destiny. The League now replied by adopting a hard line, leading to a new kind of intercommunal situation. Clashes between Hindus and Muslims in the big cities had been a feature of the last twenty years in India: but in between the occasional collapse of intercommunal relations, the communities had coexisted amicably enough. Now the sub-continent moved into a phase in which (apart from the peninsula, south of the Vindhya hills) there was something like a state of intercommunal war, even in the countryside. Yet in this situation neither Congress nor the

League took steps to propitiate the other: far from it, their mutual suspicion and enmity increased. The tension was at its height from August to November: and during these months, what there was left of the tender growth of the Cabinet Mission scheme withered, and died.

Nehru rejects grouping

July opened with the meeting of the All-India Congress Committee in Bombay to consider the action of the High Command in accepting the scheme on 25 June. There was considerable hostility from the Left Wing, but the resolution was ratified. At this session, Nehru succeeded Azad as President of the Congress. In his closing speech Nehru observed that, as far as he could see, it was not a question of the Congress accepting any plan, long or short: 'We are not bound by a single thing except that we have decided for the moment to go to the Constituent Assembly.' Asked at a press conference on 10 July what this meant, Nehru explained that the conditions laid down by the Cabinet Mission were not operative. He was specially precise in describing how the grouping provisions would be demolished:

The big probability is that from any approach to the question, there will be no grouping. Obviously, Section A will decide against grouping. Speaking in betting language, there is a 4 to 1 chance of the North-West Frontier Province deciding against grouping. Then Group B collapses. It is highly likely that Assam will decide against grouping with Bengal. . . . There is going to be finally no grouping there, because Assam will not tolerate it under any circumstances whatever. Thus you see this grouping business . . . does not get us on at all.[1]

Hitherto, the Congress leaders might have made reservations in conversation, or even in correspondence: but

[1] M. Gwyer and A. Appadorai, eds., *Speeches and Documents on the Indian Constitution 1921-47*, ii (1957), p. 613.

for Nehru to choose the first opportunity as Congress President to repudiate the grouping formula was to confirm Jinnah and his colleagues in their worst suspicions. A week later both Pethick-Lawrence and Cripps, speaking to parliament, emphasized that it was vital to their scheme for the provinces to have the opportunity to form groups if they wished. But this was insufficient to reassure the League. Against this inauspicious background, the Viceroy renewed his efforts to bring the parties into an interim government. He wrote to Nehru and Jinnah on 22 July, proposing that the balance introduced into the abortive announcement of 16 June (6 Congress, 5 Muslim League, 3 minorities) should be kept, with the political parties nominating their own candidates.

The Muslim League indignant

The Council of the League (the equivalent of the All-India Congress Committee) assembled on 27 July. The League's acceptance of the 16 May scheme was revoked (29 July) in reply to the alleged bad faith shown by the Cabinet Mission and the Congress, both over the interim government and over the grouping aspect of the scheme. 'The time has come', the Council also declared, 'for the Muslim nation to resort to direct action to achieve Pakistan', and 16 August would be observed as 'Direct Action Day'. 'This day we bid goodbye to constitutional methods', declared Jinnah. In the same spirit, Jinnah told Wavell on 31 July that the League could not accept his offer because the principle of parity had been discarded.

July also saw the carrying out of the elections for the Constituent Assembly (11–22 July) among the various provincial legislatures on a system of proportional representation. The results were on predictable lines. The Congress filled 201 of the 210 general seats, while the

League obtained all but 5 of the 78 seats reserved for Muslims.[2] The Punjab Unionist Party won 3 seats, the Communists and Dr Ambedkar's Scheduled Castes Federation 1 apiece, and there were 8 independents. The Left Wing of the Congress, led by Jayaprakash Narayan, refused to stand for the Constituent Assembly, which they denounced as a British fabrication.

The four Sikh seats remained unfilled, as the Sikh political leaders could not agree on their policy. Just before the Cabinet Mission had arrived, the major Sikh party, the Akali Dal, adopted a demand for a Sikh state, sometimes called Sikhistan or Khalistan. However, the tactics of the Sikh leaders had been little more than opportunistic. Baldev Singh, who had emerged as their accepted nominee for the interim government, was an Akali who had negotiated a pact on his party's behalf with the Unionists, and who was later to join the Congress. After writing to Attlee to complain of the lack of consideration shown to the Sikhs, Baldev Singh persuaded the different Sikh factions to accept the Cabinet Mission scheme on 14 August. The Sikhs were not able to elect their representatives to the Constituent Assembly until much later.

Meanwhile, after Jinnah declined to join the government, Wavell wrote to Nehru on 6 August inviting him to propose the names of candidates. The suggestion was made that he might discuss the situation with Jinnah, as a coalition was obviously desirable. In going beyond the basis on which it had been deemed appropriate to proceed in late June, when an interim government had been considered without Congress and built upon a League foundation, Wavell was now attempting to see if the Congress might be induced to offer assurances to the League direct, now that the making of the government

[2] Abul Kalam Azad and Abdul Ghaffar Khan were elected from the Frontier; the other three non-League Muslim seats went to the Unionists.

was in their hands. There was a certain response. On
10 August the Congress Working Committee put out a
statement designed to clarify its position *vis-à-vis* the
16 May scheme:

The Committee wish to make it clear that, while they did
not approve of all the proposals contained in this statement,
they accepted the scheme in its entirety. They interpreted it
so as to resolve the inconsistencies contained in it and fill the
omissions in accordance with the principles laid down in the
statement. They hold that provincial autonomy is a basic
provision and each province has the right to decide whether
to form or join a group or not.[3]

Even this attempt at reassurance declined into the
familiar theme that grouping was optional. Jinnah was
not therefore induced to respond to Nehru's offer of five
places in the proposed government, and after the two men
had met in Bombay on 15 August, Jinnah announced
'There will be no more meetings between me and Pandit
Nehru'.

The Calcutta killing

The next day was observed with an impressive demonstration of Muslim solidarity, but all was overshadowed
by the events in Calcutta. The Muslims formed less than
a quarter of the population of the city (497,535 out of a
total of 2,108,891) but, as in most Indian cities, were
concentrated in certain *muhallas* or wards. The Premier of
Bengal, H. S. Suhrawardy, a Muslim and a somewhat
wayward member of the League, declared 16 August a
public holiday, so that trouble might not be precipitated
by Muslim League zealots attempting to force shops and
business concerns to close, as they would on an ordinary
day. Nevertheless processions were taken out, stones were
flung, and what was later called the Great Calcutta

[3] Gwyer and Appadorai, ii. 621.

Killing (or simply The Killing) was on. The military commander, General Tuker, happened to have been called away, and the Governor, Sir Frederick Burrows, did not grasp the need to stamp out the violence as soon as it began. It was not until the 17th that the troops were called in, and only on the 18th did they effectively establish control. By then some 4,000 persons had been slain: not so much in battles between the rival mobs, as by a stab in the back in unlit alleys and lanes.

Even when order had been restored, fear remained. Week after week troops stood by, or patrolled the streets, while the press reported murder.

On 24 August it was announced that His Majesty the King-Emperor had appointed a new Executive Council, composed of the following: Nehru, Patel, Rajendra Prasad, Rajagopalachari, S. C. Bose, Jagjivan Ram, M. Asaf Ali, Syed Ali Zaheer, Sir Shafaat Ahmad Khan, Dr John Matthai, Baldev Singh, and C. H. Bhabba. The first five named were Congress Hindus, the next a Scheduled Caste Congressman, and the next two Nationalist Muslims. The remainder comprised an independent Muslim, an independent Christian, an Akali Sikh, and an independent Parsi industrialist. Thus, eight out of the twelve members belonged to the Congress.

Wavell presses for grouping

Meanwhile Lord Wavell went to Calcutta to see for himself what had happened. He was profoundly horrified to discover how far law and order had broken down. An elected ministry might be running the government of Bengal, but Wavell was, in his own estimation, responsible for the lives and property of these people as the supreme representative of British rule in India. Unless the Congress and the League could be persuaded to co-operate, the Killing would be followed by many more killings. While in Calcutta, Wavell talked to Nazimuddin, a former Premier of Bengal, and a man much respected for his piety and integrity. Nazimuddin suggested that if the Congress would bind themselves to accept the grouping provisions of the scheme, the League would reconsider its attitude. It was not perhaps altogether wise to choose this moment to put pressure on the Congress, when they were arguing that the principal responsibility for the Killing lay with the Muslim League: but Wavell was now trying to obtain the co-operation of the League. The boot was on the other foot: the Congress was not, for the moment, the obdurate party: and so it was their turn to be pressed to make a concession.

On the evening of 27 August, Wavell asked Gandhi and Nehru to meet him. He appealed to them to co-operate in reopening the path to a coalition, as the only means of bringing the sub-continent back to peace. This could be done if the grouping controversy could be settled, and so he produced a draft statement for the signature of Gandhi and Nehru. This read:

The Congress are prepared in the interests of communal harmony to accept the intention of the Statement of May 16th that provinces cannot exercise any option affecting their membership of the sections or of the groups if formed, until the decision contemplated in paragraph 19 (viii) of the Statement of May 16th is taken by the new Legislature after the new constitutional arrangements have come into operation and the first general elections have been held.

The Congress leaders refused to sign the document, and entered into many hours of what V. P. Menon (always restrained in his comments on the Congress) describes as 'legalistic arguments'.[4] The exchanges became more heated and more unavailing. Wavell indicated that

[4] Menon, p. 302.

he was not prepared to convene the Constituent Assembly unless this point was settled. He insisted that Gandhi and Nehru take away the formula for further consideration.

Why did Gandhi refuse to respond to the appeal to make a concession in the interests of communal harmony? Perhaps he was determined not to be brow-beaten: in a reply to Wavell he referred to his manner as 'minatory'. But it really appears that he did not grasp the essential nature of the problem: the lack of trust which was relentlessly growing among the leaders of the League. To him this really was a question of the legal interpretation of a quasi-legal document.

The Viceroy asked Nehru to place his formula before the Working Committee. It replied by repeating the suggestion that the question be put to the Federal Court for a judicial ruling. The Viceroy's attitude over the Constituent Assembly was resented, and lengthy arguments were deployed in favour of an early meeting.

Nehru forms a government

When the dispute was referred to the British government, they compromised by insisting that the interim government must come into action, while sanctioning the deferment of the meeting of the Constituent Assembly. It had now become standard practice to alternate the promotion of short-term objectives with the pursuit of long-term objectives. On 2 September the interim government was sworn in and began to take charge of the machinery of administration. Among the key posts, Sardar Patel became Home Minister, with additional responsibility for information and broadcasting. The Viceroy and the Cabinet Mission had wanted Patel as Home Minister: he was known as a hard man, but he was a realist and a man of his word. If the British and the

Congress were to get down to business together, then here
was a man who would strike a hard bargain—but who
was interested in actions not words. Essentially, Patel was
an administrator, and the British officials recognized him
as one of their own kind. The portfolio of Defence was
given to Baldev Singh, and for the first time the Commander-in-Chief (Field-Marshal Auchinleck) did not sit
on the Viceroy's Council. Baldev Singh was chosen as a
Sikh and a Punjabi, which together gave an impression
of a martial background: but he was essentially a political
operator, out to secure what he could for himself and his
community. Pandit Nehru became Vice-President of the
Executive Council, holding the portfolios of External
Affairs and Commonwealth Relations.

During the next six weeks Wavell devoted his main
efforts to inducing Jinnah to bring the League into the
interim government. If the situation had not been so
serious, it would have been piquant. Jinnah was desperately aware that his adversaries were gathering into their
hands the reins of government, while he looked on,
impotent; at the same time he had to negotiate to gain
some additional concession which would enable the
League to return to constitutional activity with dignity.
While Jinnah was walking this slippery path, both the
British and the Congress were aware that the non-co-
operation of the Muslims was making a mockery of the
attempt to create a free and united India. Jinnah's position was both weak and strong.

A civil war threatens

While in the greater part of India the Muslim community was a small and often frightened minority, in
Bengal and north-west India it was the majority community, able to call the political tune. This was its somewhat negative basis of power. Early in October the steady

toll of communal violence grew louder with news of intense Muslim agitation in eastern Bengal. The civil administration in Bengal was very thin on the ground, and official intelligence was completely lacking, but the press reports were sensational. The trouble centred upon Noakhali District, where Islamic fervour was always high: in mid-October reports began coming in of slaughter which might be another great killing. When the troops had gone in and restored order it was discovered that the press reports were exaggerated: at most 300 Hindus were killed by Muslim fanatics. But the background of crisis was sufficient to bring the Muslim League to realize that it must abandon its *frondeur* role and get into the government, while the British and the Congress were equally keen to bring the League into a position of responsibility. Discussion revolved around the terms of membership of the Viceroy's Council. Early in October Jinnah asked whether the Muslim League 'quota' could include a representative from the untouchables. Although taken aback, Wavell assented. The purpose of this move was to challenge the proposition for which Gandhi had fought so long—that the Depressed Castes were recognized members of the Hindu community—and also to counter the insistence of the Congress on including a Nationalist Muslim in their quota. On 13 October Jinnah wrote to Wavell indicating that 'we have decided to nominate five [members] on behalf of the Muslim League'. Wavell saw Jinnah the same day and reminded him that entry into the interim government was conditional on acceptance of the 16 May scheme. Jinnah replied that this could only be done by calling a special meeting of the Muslim League Council, the same body which had renounced the scheme. After talking to Nehru, Wavell decided to go ahead with the changes in his council, on the understanding that Jinnah had accepted the 16 May scheme.

The League joins the government

In order to accommodate the five new members, three of the previous ministers had to withdraw (two places had remained unfilled). Two Muslims resigned, but one Nationalist Muslim was retained: in his place, S. C. Bose was required to resign. The new men were regarded by Jinnah as 'sentinels' on behalf of the League. Jinnah himself did not join; he was not prepared to sit under Nehru as Vice-President of the Council. Also, Nazimuddin and Mohammad Ismail Khan, designated as ministers under the 16 June announcement, were not nominated: they were regarded as being too moderate. The League group was led by Liaqat Ali, with Abdur Rab Nishtar from the Frontier, Ghazanfar Ali Khan from Punjab, I. I. Chundrigar from Bombay, and Jogendranath Mandal from the Scheduled Castes (he had been a member of the Bengal Muslim League ministry).[5] While the League seemed to be having their way, Congress scored by refusing to give up any of the three major portfolios: External Relations, Defence, or Home Affairs. The best they would offer was the Finance Ministry, which was taken by Liaqat Ali.

The Muslim attacks upon Hindus in Noakhali were put down by the military by 20 October, but sensational press reports continued, and Gandhi's visit to the disturbed area was followed by a flood of other visitors who were less concerned to secure peace. All this had wide repercussions, and on 27 October the first incident occurred in Bihar of Hindu attacks upon Muslims. The killing rose to a peak from 1–6 November, and about 5,000 Muslims were murdered and many more driven from their homes. Both the central and the provincial ministers made efforts to stop the killing, but they had little idea of how to suppress

[5] Congress propaganda organs pointed out that Nishtar had failed to secure election in his own home province, the Frontier.

violence, once passions had been roused. Again, it was the presence of the army which brought the rising to an end.

Meanwhile Wavell's incessant reminders to Jinnah that he had not honoured the undertaking to commit the League to the 16 May scheme were parried, until on 17 November Jinnah gave a categorical reply. The Congress insisted upon its own interpretation of the scheme, which did not accept the grouping formula. In these circumstances it would be futile to summon the Muslim League Council. Because of the massacre of Muslims in Bihar, Jinnah urged that the summoning of the Constituent Assembly be postponed *sine die* while peace and order were restored.

A last effort to establish grouping

Jinnah had succeeded in creating deadlock. Wavell could proceed without the League, but this meant handing over the initiative to the Congress, who had shown little sign of compromise, while Muslim activity would inevitably pass into a phase of outright defiance, leading to complete communal breakdown and perhaps to civil war. Nehru and the Congress had been pressing for the Constituent Assembly to be convened, and the provisional date of 9 December had been fixed: almost five months after the elections for the Assembly had taken place. On 20 November the Viceroy issued invitations to the members of the Assembly: Jinnah instructed the Muslim League members not to participate, and emphasized that the Bombay resolution of 29 July still held good. Wavell therefore called upon Liaqat Ali and his colleagues to resign unless the League accepted the scheme. Liaqat Ali would not budge: he was ready to resign, but not to make any long-term commitment. Wavell therefore cabled to Pethick-Lawrence, reviving a proposal that he made

during the impasse at the end of August—that the Indian
leaders should fly to London to confront the Cabinet
Mission and the Viceroy once again on the meaning of the
grouping proposals. It was necessary to move fast, if there
was to be a meeting of the Constituent Assembly on
9 December. Wavell, on behalf of the British government,
invited Nehru and Patel, Jinnah and Liaqat Ali, and also
Baldev Singh for the Sikhs, to attend a conference in
London. At first there were refusals, but finally all except
Patel agreed to go.

Patel and partition

The role of Patel at this time is the most difficult to
follow.[6] He had the reputation of being the most bitterly
opposed to the Muslims of all the Congress leaders. He
had been a candidate for the Congress Presidency in July
1946, but Gandhi, Azad, and others of a mediating outlook had placed their influence behind Nehru. Previously
Patel had dismissed Jinnah as the leader of a fringe group
whom the Congress could deal with after they had elimina-
ted the British: but as a realist, and from his position of
vantage as Home Minister, Patel now saw that the
Congress power to dominate events was waning. The
Punjab was a melting-pot; the Frontier, though seemingly
held by the Khan brothers, was nobody's bailiwick. The
British, though unable to determine policy in India, were
not prepared to abdicate to the Congress. All this implied
that Congress must concede some form of Pakistan—at
any rate in the north-west—in order to obtain power. The
dilemma was how to carry out a division of India while
Nehru, Gandhi, and the Congress Left Wing were abso-

[6] Throughout this work the author relies for his narrative upon material
which is capable of being checked in some way. The paragraph which
follows is exceptional, relying entirely upon the evidence of an Indian
friend of great eminence who was a close spectator of the events described.

lutely opposed to this course: and how also to do this (while
conceding the bare minimum to the League), before the
current unrest degenerated into chaos. During December
Patel began to make his dispositions. He established a close
liaison with V. P. Menon, the Reforms Commissioner, and
listened without prejudice to his plan for the demission of
power via Dominion status to one or two dominions (this
constitutional conception, abhorrent to Nehru, aroused no
inhibitions in Patel). How to register an impact upon
British thinking? At this time, written communications,
however confidential, were liable to leak out. While
dissociating himself from Nehru's journey to London,
Patel sent his own emissary, Sudhir Ghosh, to make contact with Pethick-Lawrence and indicate that progress
might be made via the Dominion status formula. But
Pethick-Lawrence had listened to so many confidential
verbal offers which had come to nothing; and he paid little
attention to this overture.

Before these behind-the-scenes gestures were initiated,
the four Indian leaders and the Viceroy had flown to
London for talks which opened on 4 December. The
previous exercise in constitution-making had been widely
extended, both in time and in the subjects explored. The
December conference was highly intensive: a high-pres-
sure search for a solution of the single, vexed, grouping
proposition. The mood of the participants who had arrived
from India reflected their varying frustrations. The Viceroy had been engaged in negotiation with the Indian
leaders and with the British government for eighteen
months without relief: and he had not secured a firm
engagement anywhere. He was determined to register
upon the British government an awareness that the sands
were running out; a final decision had to be taken. Jinnah,
the professional negotiator and advocate, had virtually
lost faith in the precepts of a lifetime. If nothing was left

to the Muslims but to go down fighting, then that was what they would do. Nehru was a dreamer half awake. The dream of his political life—an India carving out its own destiny—was on the brink of realization; yet with power in his hands for the first time, he was prevented from fulfilling his dreams. Jinnah was disgruntled and uncompromising. Nehru was at first suave, and then almost indifferent to the proceedings. The Viceroy, as always, had grasped the fundamentals of the problem with sagacity and vision; but he was able to give his views their proper emphasis only by adopting what Gandhi had called his 'minatory' tone. The role of the Cabinet Ministers had changed somewhat. Pethick-Lawrence was kindly, wise, but perhaps more tired, less the recognized senior statesman. Cripps, as fertile as ever in propounding solutions, was aware of the intractable nature of the problem, and compelled by his own integrity to recognize that socialism and nationalism had not given Congress the right to take over India. Alexander—still sturdily opposed to highhandedness, and mindful of the British mission in India—was less able to put across the message that there must be no unworthy surrender of responsibility. Over these men presided the Prime Minister, Clement Attlee; an Indian specialist himself, making his own assessments, often shrewd, occasionally wrong-headed; perhaps more determined than any to see the Indian problem through in a way that would fitly conclude the past while opening up the future.

Grouping expires

During the three days 4–6 December, the negotiation with the Indian leaders was conducted in parallel; relations had reached the point where they could not be prevailed on to share their problems with each other.

Nehru's position was that of a man who saw his goal in sight and would not be deflected. He was not interested in discussing constitutional contrivances. He was not interested in conciliating the League: the Muslims would come in anyway, sooner or later, if the Constituent Assembly went ahead. The question of interpreting the meaning of the 16 May scheme could be left to the Federal Court; the only other test was the test of battle. Jinnah indicated that there was no hope of obtaining agreement on the Cabinet Mission scheme. He now seemed to detect that the League could not hope to dominate the whole six Muslim-majority provinces with their sizeable Hindu and Sikh communities. These would be able to sabotage the constitution-making in the north-west and eastern sections. When Alexander assured him that the British would not allow the Congress to force through its version of the constitution, Jinnah retorted that things had gone too far for Britain to hold back. The function of the British parliament now was only to register decisions taken in India (a profound anticipation of coming events). When Cripps returned to the original point of the conference and asked if the League would accept the 16 May scheme if Congress would accept the Cabinet Mission's view of the procedure in the sections, Jinnah replied obliquely that the chances were that they might accept. Baldev Singh, the provincial politician conscripted as national statesman, succinctly revealed the dilemma of the Sikhs under the scheme. To preserve their identity, they would have to align with Congress at the centre, while co-operating with the League in Group B: and they could not do both.

Meanwhile the Cabinet Ministers and the Viceroy were conducting their own examination of the significance of the prevailing events and trends. Cripps proposed that the British government make an explicit statement of their intentions. Wavell concurred; the British government should say what they were going to do, and then carry out their intent, without further argument. The implication of this alarmed Pethick-Lawrence; could this mean an announcement that Britain would be leaving India by some specified date? But if the British intended to stay in India, they would have to remain for ten or twenty years and perhaps put 10,000 persons into gaol. Turning to the immediate dilemma of the grouping controversy, supposing that the Federal Court should give a decision in line with the Congress interpretation and against the intention of the Cabinet Mission: could the British government accept a constitution drafted in a manner which was directly opposed to their intentions? In Wavell's opinion, the government could no longer say they would not accept a constitution unless they were prepared to face a revolution. This brought the ministers back to their main concern.

Alexander believed that they had an obligation to remain in India until a solution satisfactory to all had been found; but this view found little support. On the contrary, Cripps urged that there was a strong case for a declaration that Britain would stay on for only a strictly limited period. Wavell supported Cripps: the British had, during the latter months, found themselves no longer masters of the situation. Rather than continue to exercise nominal power while not able to enforce British authority it was more honourable to withdraw while some initiative remained. Once again, Wavell outlined his plan for a staged withdrawal, evacuating the main Hindu areas and concentrating on Calcutta and Karachi. Attlee again made the obvious comment that this would concede Pakistan to the Muslims. Cripps brushed aside a phased withdrawal. Better to see whether the Constituent Assembly would produce an acceptable constitution; and if no agreement emerged, hand over power as best proved possible. Alexander resisted this proposal with another reminder of the pledges which had been given to the minorities that Britain would not leave them in the lurch. It seemed that all the alternatives were so unacceptable that a conclusion must be postponed. What united almost all British thought was a feeling that Britain could not as a deliberate act of policy divide up India. They were also united in the conviction that Britain must not try to put back the clock; in sum, nothing except the agreement of the Indian leaders on their own future would do. But this eluded them all.

Wavell is isolated

The frustration which was shared by the Viceroy and the Cabinet aggravated the mutual sense of tension. Wavell was hampered by his own precise and proper conception of the relationship between the professional chief and the political head. He believed it was his duty to take responsibility for the execution of policy, but that it was the Cabinet Ministers' duty to lay down a clear policy for him to follow. His own experience over the grouping controversy might have revealed the difficulty of defining policy in advance: but this did not prevent him calling, ever more insistently, for a definition of policy. In a letter to King George VI, written two months later, Wavell recapitulated his own alternative plans of action. He informed the King: 'I failed, after many hours of conference, to get any definite policy from Your Majesty's Government. Their chief difficulty was reluctance to face Parliament with any proposal which would make it clear that we were withdrawing our control very shortly.'[7]

Even though the London conference had apparently exhausted all alternatives, Attlee was by no means convinced that unilateral withdrawal was the inevitable conclusion. Many years later, he referred to Wavell's attitude

[7] Wheeler-Bennett, p. 708.

at this time as 'pretty defeatist'.[8] This was a somewhat ill-considered assessment; but it is not difficult to see why the Viceroy's Cassandra-like warnings had seemed to indicate an acceptance of breakdown as inevitable. On 17 December Attlee placed before King George VI the name of Earl Mountbatten of Burma as a candidate for the viceroyalty. Not since Ellenborough, one hundred years before, had a Governor-General been replaced before his period of office elapsed. But Attlee was undoubtedly right to take this course. 'Back or sack' is a hard maxim, but the only right policy as between statesmen and their lieutenants in positions of critical importance. The Labour government had ceased to back Wavell; the only alternative was to sack him.

After grouping: the League opts out

Meanwhile the consequences of the final failure to bring together Congress and the League had to be worked out. A communiqué was issued immediately the conference closed.[9] This rehearsed once again the nature of the controversy over the 16 May scheme, especially paragraph 19 (v) and (viii). The government intimated that they had taken advice from an eminent English legal authority who confirmed that the statement said what the Cabinet Mission said it did: that the decision on grouping would be taken by a simple majority within the A, B, and C sections, and that provinces could not opt out unilaterally. The nub of the matter came in the concluding paragraph:

There has never been any prospect of success for the Constituent Assembly except upon the basis of an agreed procedure. Should the Constitution come to be framed by a Constituent Assembly in which a large section of the Indian population

---

[8] Francis Williams, *A Prime Minister Remembers* (1961), p. 209.

[9] *India; Statement by His Majesty's Government*, 6 *December*, 1946 (Gwyer and Appadorai, ii. 661).

had not been represented, His Majesty's Government could not, of course, contemplate—as the Congress have stated they would not contemplate—forcing such a Constitution upon any unwilling parts of the country.

The Constituent Assembly met on 9 December, as arranged, but none of the Muslim League members attended. Nehru moved an Objectives Resolution which declared that the new constitution would be dedicated to the goal of social revolution: but there was only the broadest attempt to specify what kind of framework this would entail.[10] M. R. Jayaker moved an amendment that the Assembly adjourn so as to allow representatives from the League and the Princely States to participate. This was agreed, and the Assembly adjourned until 20 January. And so 1946 came to an end in a kind of limbo, as regards policy-making, both in New Delhi and in London.

[10] Const. Ass. Deb., vol 1, no. 4, p. 57.

6

Mountbatten Works Out a Deal
(February-May 1947)

Two months were to pass between Attlee's actual decision to replace Wavell by Mountbatten and the public announcement of the change-over; another month passed before Mountbatten took charge in India. This was also a time when Pethick-Lawrence was (in his own words) at the end of his tether. He found it hard to accept a policy of committing Britain to quit India by an arbitrary date: but (as his obituary in *The Times* was to observe) the Prime Minister and Sir Stafford Cripps had taken matters of high policy in respect to India very much into their own hands with scant regard to the views of the India Office. On 2 April, a few days after Mountbatten reached Delhi, Pethick-Lawrence tendered his resignation; he was succeeded by Lord Listowel, who had already taken a close interest in India. During the three months from mid-December to mid-March the implementation of Indian policy was, as it were, in the pending tray.

From 9 to 27 January Attlee was much occupied in negotiating with Aung San over the future of Burma. The successful outcome demonstrated that independence was to be had for the asking by a determined and single-minded leader who could demonstrate strong national leadership.

On his return to India, Wavell (who, of course, had no inkling of his coming dismissal) gave the British government a flat ultimatum: they must accept a terminal date for British rule in India, in order to wind up the army and the civil service effectively. After consideration, he stipulated 31 March 1948 as the latest date by which the transfer of power should be carried out.[1] This was accepted by the British government, which was proceeding with their own calculations in consort with the Viceroy-designate.

Mountbatten: the modern prince

The brilliant personality of Earl Mountbatten of Burma so dominates the closing chapter of British rule in India that some kind of character sketch is required. As Chief of Combined Operations and Supreme Commander in South East Asia, he was given appointments fraught with difficulty. In these activities, improvisation was an essential ingredient. In building up his forces to win the victory, morale was the key. In South East Asia there was a foundation of failure. Mountbatten moved among his men (in sharp contrast to the unseen commanders before him), projecting confidence by displays of dynamic decision: and also by listening to all he met. His enemies called him a showman (and he seems to have induced intense admiration or intense dislike among those who had close contact with him), but there was much more: a capacity to impose his will upon events. He showed himself both traditional and modern. He carried his royal connexion with style and dignity; but new ideas, new techniques, new technology were exploited for all they were worth. Perhaps his most surprising trait was an ability to communicate with the new nationalist leaders of Asia. He had sensed that the morose and unprepossessing Aung San was the key to Burmese politics; and at a time when some of his advisers

[1] Wheeler-Bennett, p. 708.

wanted to try Aung San as a traitor and a murderer, Mountbatten was insisting on treating him as the representative of the new Burma. British royalty had not been noticeable for its radical tendencies, and Mountbatten's disposition to encourage the new revolutionary Asian nationalism was resented by those who conceived that royal personages should stick to precedent and protocol. It was his imaginative radicalism which induced Mountbatten to respond to Attlee's offer of the viceroyalty. But he was not going to step aside from his cherished naval career in order to become the British government's chief servant in India, as Wavell had been. He demanded an effective voice in carrying out the role of the 'Last Viceroy' as he saw himself: not sadly, but gladly.[2]

During the month of January Mountbatten discussed the terms on which he would go out to India. He hoped that he might go at the invitation of the Indian leaders, but this was deemed impracticable. Determined that his selection should be understood as having a special significance he pressed for a specific statement, that Britain was leaving India, to accompany the announcement of his appointment. This, of course, coincided with the view of Cripps and with the stand taken by Wavell. He resisted the introduction of any 'escape clause'. He also resisted a proposal by Cripps that he should accompany the new Viceroy to India and assist him to break the political deadlock. Mountbatten had no intention of becoming a *roi fainéant*, and he countered with the suggestion that Cripps should take over as Secretary of State. In his dry way Attlee dismissed this as neither necessary nor advisable.[3]

---

[2] To write in the past tense about a living person may appear appropriate only when one is contributing to *The Times* morgue. But whatever its limitations, this essay is conceived as a historical study.

[3] Williams, p. 217.

British policy defined

Mountbatten asked for a directive from the Cabinet: a mandate, as it were. He did not receive this, but instead he was given a letter immediately before he departed in March. Some of the key passages in this letter were as follows:

It is the definite objective of His Majesty's Government to obtain a unitary Government for British India and the Indian States, if possible within the British Commonwealth, through the medium of a Constituent Assembly, set up and run in accordance with the Cabinet Mission's Plan. ... If by 1 October you consider that there is no prospect of reaching a settlement on the basis of a unitary Government ... you should report to His Majesty's Government on the steps which you consider should be taken for the handing over of power on the due date. ...

The date fixed for the transfer of power is a flexible one to within one month but you should aim at 1 June, 1948 as the effective date for the transfer of power. ...

It is essential that there should be the fullest co-operation with the Indian leaders in all steps that are taken as to the withdrawal of British power so that the process may go forward as smoothly as possible. ...

You should take every opportunity of stressing the importance of ensuring that the transfer of power is effected with full regard to the defence requirements of India. In the first place you will impress upon the Indian leaders the great importance of avoiding any breach in the continuity of the Indian Army and of maintaining the organisation of defence on an all-Indian basis. Secondly, you will point out the need for continued collaboration in the security of the Indian Ocean areas for which provision might be made in an agreement between the two countries. ...[4]

[4] This letter was, of course, classified as Top Secret, but it has been printed in various publications: for example Michael Edwardes, in *The Last Years of British India*, reproduces the letter in full on pp. 146–7.

Meanwhile, in India, the Congress made another effort to reassure the League over the grouping procedure. On 5 January 1947 the All-India Congress Committee passed a long resolution, in which the vital paragraph was as follows:

The AICC is anxious that the Constituent Assembly should proceed with the work of framing a constitution for free India with the goodwill of all the parties concerned and, with a view to removing the difficulties that have arisen owing to varying interpretations, agree to advise action in accordance with the interpretation of the British Government in regard to the procedure to be followed in the sections.

Even in this effort at conciliation, it appeared to be impossible to state an unequivocal proposition, and the resolution went on to insert a caveat about the right of the provinces to make their own decisions—including the right of minorities, such as the Sikhs, to their own viewpoint. And so the last paragraph stated that 'in the event of any attempt at such compulsion, a province or part of a province has the right to take such action as may be deemed necessary in order to give effect to the wishes of the people concerned'. If the Congress had made such a declaration in May 1946, or in August, or even in December 1946, this would have been sufficient to break the deadlock. But timing is everything in politics; and the Congress sense of timing between 1939 and 1947 was hardly ever right. By now Jinnah and the League had perceived that more was to be gained by intransigence than by conciliation. A curious kind of equation seemed to have been formed: within the trio—British, Congress, League—only one party at a time could opt out, could be intractable. It was necessary for the other two to come to terms. Perhaps a really Machiavellian British government, discovering this formula, might at this stage have introduced a programme of repression, and thus induced the Congress and the League to come to terms, to co-operate against the

British! In fact, of course, because the Congress had been intransigent too early to be effective, they now had to concede the initiative to the obstructions of the League.

Jinnah refused to acknowledge that the Congress resolution of 5 January was an outright acceptance of the Cabinet Mission scheme. The Congress had hoped by its gesture to bring the League into the Constituent Assembly: but when it met again on 20 January the Muslims absented themselves. As February opened, the Congress tried to return to pressure techniques: and failed. On 5 February all the Congress and minority members of the interim government wrote to Wavell demanding the resignation of the League members, in view of their outright refusal to accept the 16 May scheme. Liaqat replied with the familiar counter-charges against the Congress. On 13 February Nehru reiterated the demand for the resignation of the League ministers, and two days later Patel told the press that the Congress members would withdraw unless the matter was settled. Wavell was aware of the forthcoming announcement of the intention to set a final date to British rule (though he did not know of the sting in its tail) and he persuaded Nehru and Patel to await the new development.

Attlee's statement to parliament on 20 February began by recapitulating the efforts made to secure agreement on the Cabinet Mission scheme. He then sprang the big surprise: to end the uncertainty, British rule would terminate, come what may, 'by a date not later than June 1948'. The customary appeal to the leaders to sink their differences was followed by the ominous conclusion:

If it should appear that such a constitution [in conformity with the scheme] will not have been worked out by a fully representative Assembly before [June 1948], His Majesty's Government will have to consider to whom the powers of the Central Government in British India should be handed over . . .

whether as a whole to some form of central Government for British India or in some areas to the existing Provincial Governments, or in such other ways as may seem most reasonable and in the best interests of the Indian people.[5]

This statement created more uncertainty than had existed before: on what legal basis could a British government proceed with these undefined options? An Act of Parliament might regularize the process whereby hundreds of millions of persons and thousands of square miles of territory formerly under the British Crown were put up for auction, as it were: but no Act of Parliament could transform the provinces or 'some other' units into newly sovereign states. Moreover, the double insistence that any constitution, to secure British recognition, must be agreed by a 'fully representative Assembly' was an invitation to the Muslim League to stand aside and in due time demand their rights when the Congress Assembly presented their constitution.

Congress reactions

The announcement that Wavell would be succeeded by Mountbatten aroused varying speculation. In Congress circles it was proclaimed that Wavell had been pro-Muslim and anti-Congress. Mountbatten was known to have established cordial relations with Nehru. This reading of the situation implied that after the change-over the Muslim League would be cut down to size, while Congress inherited the kingdom. The truth was that Wavell had consistently opposed any dismemberment of India, while within a few weeks Mountbatten had conceded the inevitability of Pakistan. However, the record of the transfer of power was translated into myth and legend even while events were being enacted: and the actual significance of the contributions of Wavell and his successor to indepen-

[5] *Indian Policy: Statement of 20th February,* 1947, Cmd. 7047.

dence-making in South Asia have seldom been objectively examined.

Attlee's announcement drew from Nehru a statesman-like response. He said:

It is a challenge to all of us and we shall try to meet it bravely in the spirit of that challenge. I trust that we shall endeavour to get out of the ruts and end the internal conflicts that have frustrated our efforts and delayed our advance . . .

Brave words: but the rut which at one time divided Congress and the League had become a chasm. A Congress resolution on the announcement of 20 February asked for the recognition of the interim government as a Dominion government. This status, which had been suspected as a device for perpetuating British control, was beginning to be seen as a stepping-stone to full independence. The resolution accepted the rule of 'no compulsion' to areas which did not join the Constituent Assembly. The resolution went on: 'In the Punjab it is necessary to find a way out which involves the least amount of compulsion. This would necessitate the division of the Punjab into two provinces. . . . The Working Committee commend this solution.'

Storm in the Punjab

Recognition that the vision of Indian unity must take account of the drab reality of communal discord was underlined by the political crisis which finally ended the not ignoble attempt by the founders of the Punjab Unionist Party to unite rival faiths in a common bid to raise themselves up. After the death of Sikander Hyat Khan, the Unionists had dwindled into a party of memory. The squalid conspiracy to keep out the Muslim League which had staved off the demise of the Unionists in 1946 could no longer conceal the divisions between the communities. In Bengal and Bihar the communal riots had begun because *goondas* or professional hooligans had exploited the tension for their own profit. The mobs had been joined by other jackals, who indulged in rioting: but when authority stamped upon the *goondas*, the violence abated. In Punjab the situation was, potentially, more dangerous because the whole population were of a turbulent, warlike disposition. In January the Premier banned the Muslim League National Guards and the Hindu Rashtriya Swayamsevak Sangh (RSS): partly to forestall the revival of the militant Sikh Akali Sena, disbanded the previous year. Far from quelling the militants, the ban was the signal for a League civil-disobedience movement which stretched the police resources to the limit. The Premier, Sir Khizr Hyat Khan Tiwana (leader of the Congress–Sikh coalition, in which his own Muslim Unionists were a tiny rump), recognized that there was no longer any purpose in his balancing act: on 2 March he resigned. He stated that the urgency imparted to the situation by the statement of 20 February necessitated a genuine coalition government for Punjab, including the League. The Governor invited the provincial League leader (the Khan of Mamdot) to form a ministry, but the Sikh and Congress groups refused to co-operate. Without their goodwill the League could not govern, or even function as a minority government: and so on 5 March the Governor took over direct responsibility for the province under Section 93 of the 1935 Act. Rioting broke out in Lahore on 4 March, and civil strife continued throughout the province until 21 March. Then followed an uneasy lull.

British policy becomes obsolete

The letter which Attlee had given to Mountbatten reflected none of this. Indeed, almost none of the guide-lines enumerated therein ever became even remotely relevant. The goal of a united India; the cut-off date for a decision on unity or partition (1 October, 1947); the date for transfer of power (1 June, 1948); the smooth co-operation between the parties; the continuity of the armed forces; the treaty for defence co-operation: not one of these conditions was fulfilled. Even before his departure, Mountbatten could see clearly enough the contrast between the crisis atmosphere, and the ideal terms for transfer by agreement which the British government postulated. Mountbatten therefore asked for an apprecia-tion of the situation which would arise in the event of a transfer of power to more than one authority: so clearly envisaged in the 20 February statement. Obviously, the India Office had been required to consider this contin-gency. Because of the continual emphasis upon the provinces as sovereign units, there was a tendency to think of these as the 'residuary legatees' of British power. But the dangers and difficulties inherent in such a con-clusion led the experts to insist that division was to be preferred to fragmentation. Congress was being drawn inexorably to recognize that separate Muslim states might become inevitable; but it might be expected to try to work for their restriction to areas which could not hope to main-tain an independent existence, except for a short period. The alternatives which had been principally under dis-cussion were (*a*) the full six provinces of Pakistan; (*b*) the same, subject to the partitioning of Bengal and Assam and Punjab; (*c*) Pakistan minus Assam; (*d*) Pakistan, minus Bengal and Assam.

There was nothing in all this that an intelligent spec-tator could not deduce for himself. What must have struck Lord Mountbatten as most important was that the approach of the Labour government remained empirical. No solution was ruled out, and no particular solution was favoured, if, as now seemed so probable, the vision of a united India had to be relinquished.[6]

Mountbatten finds no compromise

The new Viceroy began with the established technique of a marathon of interviews with all the leaders. To his jaded visitors, Mountbatten offered a glimpse of energy and a sense of purpose and drive which most of them had long since forfeited. One of the most remarkable exchanges was with Gandhi, who advanced once again his proposal for a gesture of conciliation, whereby Jinnah would be given entire responsibility for leading a government of his own choice. To his previous plan, Gandhi added the rider that the Congress Party would guarantee to co-operate fairly and sincerely. Mountbatten was to be the sole umpire in any dispute about whether the Jinnah government was acting in the interests of the whole Indian people. Gandhi went on to make an appeal to Mountbatten to stay and govern the new India as the chosen head of the state, dedicating his life to the service of the Indian people. All this was a lot for the newly-arrived Viceroy to swallow; and, as it turned out, it was more than the Congress was ready to swallow. This was Gandhi's last great intervention in the search for agreement among the Indian leaders.[7] Once again, if this spirit of generosity had been in evidence the previous summer, it might have made all the difference. Now it was too late.

When Mountbatten met Jinnah, he recognized that this was the man who held the key to the whole Indian problem. Jinnah's analysis was, in its own way, as radical as

[6] It should, perhaps, be made quite clear that this is a deductive statement. The author has not made an approach to Lord Mountbatten for his version of events. It would not have been easy to preserve objectivity, if one took one's narrative from the central character in the story.

[7] See the present author's *Reorientations; Studies on Asia in Transition* (1965), pp. 145–7.

that of Gandhi: a 'surgical operation', the dissection of India. In a memorable phrase he declared 'I do not care how little you give me so long as you give it to me completely'. The frustrations of the last months had brought Jinnah, like others, a certain catharsis. At one time he had bitterly opposed a 'motheaten' Pakistan. Now he saw that more important to the Muslims than bidding for the maximum area of control was to ensure that, whatever house they gained, they were masters in their own house. If the Muslims were to be denied mastery over their own affairs, then they would resist to the death.

Compared with these two speakers in strange tongues, Nehru came to Mountbatten as a modern man, with whom he could communicate. Among his staff and colleagues, Mountbatten had no use for 'yes men'. He was always asking: what is your solution? How would you deal with this situation? So now he asked Nehru how he would tackle the Indian problem. Nehru answered that it would not be right to impose a settlement upon a community which was in a majority in a specific area. He was therefore in favour of each province—and in the case of Punjab and Bengal, the two parts of these provinces—being given the right to decide.

A deal takes shape

This, at any rate, was one of the voices with which Nehru spoke, though he had a deceptive capacity to give his listener the impression that their minds were as one, when a gulf divided them.

Mountbatten had arrived with a mind open to any solution that would be acceptable to political India. His first weeks were spent in assuring his visitors that he had not come with the blueprint of a new plan, and that the Cabinet Mission scheme remained the best solution. Very rapidly he had to pass into the second phase of activity, the evolution of his own New Deal. As Mountbatten was to observe later, his plan

was created by the processes of open diplomacy. Its every stage and every point was the result of planned discussion with all the leaders. The plan was not put on paper for several weeks but I kept notes, and at every turn I spoke and tried to reconcile the different points of view and gain points of common ground.[8]

His interview with Nehru, in which a specific acknowledgement of the inevitability of partition seemed to have been reached, was followed within a week by a conference with the provincial governors. On the eve of the conference, the broad principles of a Deal had been evolved:

1. The proposals were designed to place the responsibility of dividing India conspicuously on the Indians themselves.

2. The provinces should have the right to determine their own future. This would mean that the provinces already substantially participating in the Constituent Assembly (Madras, Bombay, United Provinces, Central Provinces, Bihar, Orissa, Assam) would confirm that they wished to continue functioning through the Assembly.

3. In Bengal and Punjab, the representatives of the Muslim-majority districts and those of the other districts, sitting separately, would be asked to determine their own future.

4. Sylhet District in Assam would be given the option to join a partitioned Bengal, if this should emerge under (3).

5. A fresh general election would be held in the North-West Frontier Province, where a political stalemate existed.

[8] *Address by Earl Mountbatten to the East India Association, 29 June 1948.*

6. The Muslim-majority provinces, and the Muslim-majority districts of the partitioned provinces would be given the option of joining a new Constituent Assembly.[9]

The Governors gave the Viceroy some idea of the storm which was gathering across northern India. On the Frontier, Khan Ghaffar Khan had created a new militia with pistols and red uniforms; in reply, the Muslim League had raised a force of 'Green Shirts'; new elections were imperative, to determine the direction in which popular feeling was flowing. The demands of the Sikhs were growing in Punjab, and if there was a show-down, a number of army divisions would be needed to quell the disorder. On the other side of India, there was trouble brewing on the Bengal–Assam border, where League national guards (the Ansars) were preparing for a struggle over Sylhet. In Calcutta there were even clashes within the police force between the Gurkhas who had long provided the riot squads and the Punjabi Mussalmans whom Suhrawardy had imported. Because Calcutta was the focus of a commercial hinterland which included Muslim- and Hindu-majority areas, it would be beneficial to try to gain agreement for the metropolis to be under joint control in case of a partition. But perhaps it might be possible to find an acceptable scheme for a united Bengal? This raised the question of whether provinces should have the option of remaining independent, as well as deciding for Hindustan or Pakistan. Provinces which might choose to exercise this option would be Punjab and Bengal: in which case it would be necessary to permit a preliminary vote on this question before deciding on partition.

Congress acquiesces in partition

While the Deal for the future was being drafted and re-drafted by the Viceroy and his personal team of assistants,

[9] Alan Campbell-Johnson, *Mission with Mountbatten* (1951), p. 62.

the work of the interim government had to go forward.
Liaqat Ali as Finance Minister introduced a budget which
bore heavily upon big business. There was a tax of 25 per
cent on all profits over Rs100,000, a capital gains tax, and
measures against tax evasion. Nehru had called for
measures against the war profiteers, but several Congress
ministers protested strongly against a tax policy designed
to hit the millionaire backers of Congress. Another crisis
passed over in a more encouraging way. There was cla-
mour in the central legislature to release all sentenced
members of the INA. Wavell had vetoed this, and now
Mountbatten induced Nehru to stand up in the Assembly
and reject the demand. The League upheld this stand.
Here was a small sign that the leaders understood that
they were entering an era in which they could no longer
utilize grievances against the British as a substitute for
positive decision-making. In one of his encounters with
the Viceroy, Patel told him bluntly: 'You won't govern
yourself and you won't let the central government
govern. . . . Let us govern.'[10] Patel believed that if the
British would go, the arguing would stop and the race
would go to the strong. Dominion status, as V. P. Menon
had indicated, might provide a means to mollify British
susceptibilities about Empire and Commonwealth, and
at the same time provide a constitutional formula whereby
the interim government under the 1935 Act could transform itself into a sovereign government. Patel wanted
power soon, before events got out of hand. While the
Viceroy devised his Deal, Patel busied himself in fixing
the Congress so that the 'extreme' elements—the Left
Wing, the Gandhians, and Hindu orthodoxy—were out-
manoeuvred by the organization men of the centre who,
like Patel, knew that the business of a government is to
govern. The formal expression of this fixing of the Congress

[10] cf. Campbell-Johnson, p. 72.

by Patel was given in a statement which Rajendra Prasad made on 28 April as President of the Constituent Assembly:

While we have accepted the Cabinet Mission's Statement of May 16, 1946, which contemplated the Union of the different provinces and States within the country, it may be that the Union may not comprise all provinces. If that unfortunately comes to pass, we shall have to be content with a constitution for a part of it. In that case, we can and should insist that one principle will apply to all parts of the country and no constitution will be forced upon any unwilling part of it. This may mean not only a division of India, but a division of some provinces. For this we must be prepared and the Assembly may have to draw up a constitution based on such division.[11]

The Deal taken to London

In a sense, the drama that was now to be enacted was a pageant that was not real life. A great deal would happen in the next month before Congress and the League gave their assent to the Mountbatten Deal. But behind the centre of the stage, where so much was going on, Patel was already planning how he would make his dispositions when the curtain came down on the Act.

Meanwhile the Deal, refined after many drafts and many conferences, was ready for submission to the Cabinet. General Ismay departed for London on 2 May with the draft and prepared to discuss the Deal. Even at this stage, revision continued, and certain last-minute amendments were cabled to Ismay: for example, in the Frontier Province, a referendum was to take the place of an election as a better means of ascertaining the popular will. A referendum was not considered to be a possible method of taking

[11] Const. Ass. Deb., vol. 3, no. 1, p. 345. On the same day Nehru stated that "there could be no coercion, except of course the coercion and compulsion of events" (ibid. p. 352).

the decision on partition in Punjab and Bengal. The alternatives—the province to join Hindustan, the province to join Pakistan, the province to be partitioned, the province to become a sovereign state—were supposed to be too complex to be determined by popular voting.

The actual method of determining the will of the people could only be an approximation to accuracy. The administrative districts—which must provide the basis for a partition—often did not coincide with the constituencies of the representatives who were to make the choice. Thus any vote for partition must be regarded as a 'notional' partition: the actual boundaries would have to be determined by a special boundary commission.

In Delhi Mountbatten was preparing the ground for the acceptance of his Deal by the party leaders. He met Gandhi and Jinnah on 3 May. Gandhi remained opposed to partition, and vainly pressed his own formula for a 'transfer of power' to Jinnah. Jinnah himself was able to discern that a division of India was coming, but in order to ensure that he was not cheated he was clamouring for the choice to be made by the people. He calculated that the untouchables and other under-privileged groups would side with the Muslims against Congress and the caste Hindus. He was reminded that the Cabinet Mission scheme held the field, and that partition was not yet, formally, the recommended solution.

After meeting the Viceroy, Gandhi and Jinnah agreed to confer together at Jinnah's Delhi residence. Gandhi once more produced the plan he had prepared to keep India together. Its main features were: (a) no division of India until after the British departed: this question would be resolved by Congress and the League, not by the British; (b) a Court of Arbitration to guarantee minority rights; (c) a homogeneous government, formed either by Congress or the League (the familiar conciliation formula);

(*d*) no referendum in NWFP and no partition in Punjab or Bengal: 'all this should be left to be done or not done after the British left'. Not surprisingly, these proposals made little appeal to Jinnah. Gandhi added:

> We did talk about Pakistan cum partition. I told him that my opposition to Pakistan persisted as before and suggested that in view of his declaration of faith in non-violence he should try to convert his opponents by reasoning with them and not by show of force. He was however quite firm. . . . Logically, and for a believer in non-violence, nothing, not even the existence of God could be outside its scope.

To Jinnah, with the end of the road in sight, this combination of unacceptable constitutional conditions and metaphysical divination was incomprehensible; he countered with a brief communiqué, in which the chief proposition ran: 'He [Gandhi] thinks that division is not inevitable, whereas in my opinion not only is Pakistan inevitable, but is the only practical solution of India's political problem.'

Another visit to Simla

The key to the success or failure of the Deal, in Mountbatten's estimation, was Jawaharlal Nehru. He could not be expected to understand that the silent strong man, Patel, had already taken the decision. Some commentators have suggested that Mountbatten was out of his depth with Patel, and it is true that he concentrated on winning over Nehru. If Mountbatten calculated that with Nehru accepting the Deal, then opposition from Gandhi would be neutralized—whereas with Nehru and Gandhi against the Deal, then no tough marshalling of forces by Patel could 'deliver' Congress support—then the Viceroy was certainly right. At any rate, Mountbatten decided that when he retired to Simla for a short break he would invite Nehru to stay at Viceregal Lodge.

Mountbatten came up to Simla on 7 May. He brought most of his personal staff with him, and also V. P. Menon. Writing at the time, or soon afterwards, the Viceroy's press attaché observed of Menon that he 'was closely involved in all the 1945 Simla and the 1946 Cabinet Mission Plan negotiations. Although he has suffered a period of eclipse he is still the trusted confidante of Vallabhbhai Patel.'[12] This seems to indicate that Mountbatten was aware of the importance of keeping close contact with Sardar Patel, although, in the light of his refusal to go to London in December, the Viceroy would know that the Sardar was inimical to the personal contacts in which Nehru (at his best) was so impressive and engaging.

With Nehru came the man who in Mountbatten's scheme of things had a role similar to that of V. P. Menon with Patel: Krishna Menon, Nehru's confidant. It was another mark of the Viceroy's freedom from conventional prejudices that he accepted Krishna Menon when before and since this man has been anathema to the Establishments of every persuasion (he had even been expelled from the British Labour Party).

The day after the Viceroy and his party arrived at Simla, they were joined by Nehru and Krishna Menon. There were desultory discussions of diverse points. Nehru still clung to the illusion that the Frontier was a Congress province, and therefore objected to the proposal for a referendum. However, on the positive side, there were indications that the new India would be ready to stay in the Commonwealth and to accept Dominion status, at any rate for a period. This status could become operative before the terminal date (June 1948) announced on 20 February: it should take place during 1947.[13]

---

[12] Campbell-Johnson, p. 85.
[13] Ibid., p. 87.

By Saturday, 10 May, Mountbatten had received the reactions of the Cabinet to his Deal. A few verbal amendments had been included in order to clarify the presentation of the case, in addition to the referendum in the Frontier Province. Confident that he could now press ahead, the Viceroy issued a communiqué announcing that he would be meeting the leaders of Congress, the League, and the Sikhs, and also representatives of the Princes on the following Saturday, 17 May, 'to present to them the plan which His Majesty's Government has now made for the transfer of power to Indian hands'. Mountbatten's technique was different from that employed by the Cabinet Mission and Wavell. They had first invited argument over their scheme; and then, when implacable divisions appeared between the parties, published the scheme for a further argument to be conducted in public. Mountbatten had discussed the overall problem with the leaders; he had outlined his Deal for their preliminary study, and now he was about to publish the Deal as a virtual Award. There was to be no manoeuvering for party advantage at any stage, either in public or private: although the greatest possible care had been taken to discuss the Deal from every angle.

Crisis again

Now, amid the scented pines and twinkling lights of the Simla hills, Mountbatten relaxed before the great day when the destiny of India would be resolved. Acting on impulse, he decided to allow Nehru a preliminary look at the Plan: considering him not so much as one of the principal protagonists, but as a friend whose comment would be welcome. Mountbatten has stated that he had an 'absolute hunch' that the redraft from London might not be accepted by Congress. On the Saturday evening,

Nehru began to read the draft of the Viceroy's Deal. His extraordinary response was to put everybody into a state of confusion—Viceroy, Prime Minister, and all—until some three weeks later the crisis was resolved.

7

The Deal Rejected, and Accepted
(May-June 1947)

Oᴺ the afternoon of Sunday, 11 May, Nehru handed the Viceroy a long note containing his reactions to the new Deal. This provides a remarkable revelation of his baffling personality. He wrote:

I have read the draft proposals you gave me with the care they deserved. . . . But with all the goodwill in the world I reacted to them very strongly. Indeed they produced a devastating effect on me. The relatively simple proposals that we had previously discussed now appeared, in the garb that HMG had provided for them, in an entirely new context which gave them an ominous meaning. . . . The picture of India that emerged frightened me. In fact, much that we had done so far was undermined, and the Cabinet Mission's scheme and subsequent developments were set aside and an entirely new picture presented—a picture of fragmentation and conflict and disorder . . . HMG seem to function in an ivory tower of their own, isolated from realities in India. . . . If my reactions were so powerful, you can well imagine what my colleagues and others will think and feel.

When Mountbatten tried to discover what was at the bottom of this outburst, he was told that the Cabinet Mission scheme was not dead: except, in a way, to the Muslim League. The Constituent Assembly had been set up in accordance with the scheme, and was functioning (except for a few provinces). The Muslim League had joined the interim government on the basis of the scheme:

and now all was to be set aside and the 'Balkanization' of
the country forced through at the will of the British
government.[1]

What made Nehru react in this way to proposals which
embodied a plan for determining the will of the people of
India to a partition upon lines of religion, which only a
fews days before he (Nehru) had publicly recognized as
the supreme question to be answered? At the time, it
must have appeared baffling. But in after years, Nehru
was to exhibit much the same apparent amnesia in
dealing with China. During the period 1954–8, Nehru
insisted that India and China were partners in the
promotion of international peace and understanding,
despite all the indications of China's expansionist border
intentions. During the next four years, 1958–62, he still
discounted the danger to peace; and then, when the break
came in October 1962, Nehru bitterly denounced the
treachery and deceit of China, when the expansionist
purpose of the great neighbour increasingly became
apparent. The same must have been true of the first half
of 1947. While going through the motions of consultation
and discussion with Mountbatten on a plan for partition,
he had remained entranced by the vision of a united
India. Confronted by the mechanism for partition in the
inescapable context of the written page, his first reaction
was to deny that such a development was possible.

The Deal redrafted

The situation confronted Mountbatten with several
kinds of dilemma. So far, he had been able to carry forward
the Indian leaders and the British government on the
current of his own confidence. Now, the British government, having been told that Nehru approved the Deal,

[1] Campbell-Johnson, p. 89.

and aware that only minor amendments had been inserted, would be sceptical of a fresh assurance that a plan was acceptable in India. Nehru, having been brought to the brink of accepting a plan for partition, might refuse to consider anything infringing the unity of India, and so might plunge the country into turmoil. It was the kind of situation which had confronted Wavell and the Cabinet Mission in their own Simla meeting, only twelve months before: and their solution had been to plod gamely but unprofitably on with the old rejected formula.

At this moment of crisis, Mountbatten exhibited his genius for improvisation, his resilience, his capacity to extract success out of failure. He went to work, with V. P. Menon at his side, to revise the Deal so as to overcome Nehru's objections, while preserving the essence of his plan to place the onus of dividing India upon the representatives of India themselves. First, a press statement was issued announcing the postponement of the date for presenting the Deal to the Indian leaders from 17 May to 2 June. Only the barest interval was thus allowed for getting the revised plan cleared with London. Nehru's main charge was that the Deal, as previously formulated, would lead to the Balkanization of India. The provision for the provinces already participating in the Constituent Assembly to ratify their continuing membership was deleted. This was a formality, inserted mainly to propitiate the Congress with its insistence upon provincial autonomy. The question of provinces choosing to become independent and sovereign was dropped. This had been raised to provide for Bengal, and possibly Punjab, choosing to 'go it alone'. The latter contingency was remote; and if the Bengali politicians should get together and opt for an undivided, sovereign Bengal, this could be dealt with at a later stage. This left certain minor objections to be resolved. There had been an intention to create special electoral colleges in the provinces which would have to choose between Hindustan and Pakistan, or to vote on the partition of the province. A quick calculation showed that only in the legislature of the Frontier Province was communal representation so balanced as to make a direct choice by the legislators a possible distortion of the actual numbers of the communities. But the Frontier was going to decide by referendum anyway: so Sind, Punjab, and Bengal could make their choice through the existing legislative assemblies. Nehru had also objected to the method of choice in Baluchistan: partly by tribal leaders, partly by the members of the Quetta municipality. This was admittedly a curious basis for such a decision, and it was agreed to consider a more democratic method of choice (in the end, no better means were found, so Baluchistan's destiny was decided by a group of town councillors and clan chieftains).

Nehru professed himself satisfied with these amendments; while, in addition, encouraged by Krishna Menon, he pressed for the recognition of the interim government as having Dominion status. Mountbatten—with V. P. Menon restored to his former role as constitutional consultant—proceeded to work out the implications of Dominion status and Commonwealth membership. This would simplify the handing over process, cutting out the need for a constitution to be completed before the transfer of power, and for a treaty to be negotiated, ratifying the new relationship between Britain and the successor states. A transitional form of Dominion status, based upon the 1935 Act, could be introduced before the end of 1947. This would put the responsibilities of administration into the hands of the national leaders before the administrative machinery had begun to run down, with the withdrawal of key British officials.

Mountbatten goes to London

Mountbatten had made a virtue out of the necessity to overcome Nehru's emotional crisis: once again, the reins were firmly under his control. However, in London, Ismay as Mountbatten's representative could not understand the nuances of the new initiative, and he suggested that he should return to Delhi to put himself back into the picture. The government also felt the need to catch up with the latest trend of events, and informed Mountbatten that either a minister ought to fly to Delhi or else the Viceroy ought to come to London. Mountbatten did not hesitate in the face of these alternatives. Despite the tensions in the atmosphere, and despite Nehru's suspicions of what went on in London, he elected to make the journey. He had no intention of repeating the Cabinet Mission situation, with Indian political leaders talking across him or even behind him to impressionable Cabinet Ministers.

Before he departed, Mountbatten obtained the reactions of Congress and the League to the revised Deal. Nehru wanted a referendum in Sylhet District; and this was agreed. He also wanted further modifications; which he was persuaded to withdraw. The attitude of Jinnah and the League leadership was that they could not agree to the partition of Punjab and Bengal, but that they would have to bow to the inevitable. Thus reassured, Mountbatten took off from Delhi on 18 May, and by employing long-range fuel tanks and double crews succeeded in touching down at Northolt at 10.30 a.m. the next day.

The Viceroy's encounter with the Prime Minister and the Cabinet was brisk and brief. This time, there were no amendments to the plan brought from India. The acceleration of the transfer by the introduction of Dominion status well before the end of 1947 was accepted; and the entire Deal was rapidly endorsed by the Cabinet. Mount-

batten was back in Delhi by the night of 30-31 May. His
absence had not been uneventful. Jinnah came out with a
demand for the full six-provinces Pakistan, and—in
addition—a corridor linking the east and west wings. In
reply, the Congress denounced this final demonstration
that Jinnah had never accepted the Cabinet Mission
Scheme and called upon the acting Viceroy (Sir John
Colville, Governor of Bombay) to ask Mountbatten to
abandon his Deal and impose the Scheme as an award or
settlement, meanwhile treating the interim government
as a Dominion government. And so, for Congress, the
wheel had turned full circle. Almost one year after reject-
ing the essential feature of the Scheme—grouping—they
were prepared to swallow the full Scheme in a last-
minute effort to avoid partition.

The move (like most Congress gestures) put the British
in a difficult situation; as it was now necessary to renounce
the Scheme—which had been so assiduously recommended
as the best solution—in favour of Pakistan, so vigorously
dismissed as impossible. If the worst happened, and Congress refused to accept the amended Deal, all that would
remain would be for the British government to proceed
with an emergency operation. The statement of 20
February had envisaged handing over power to the
provinces as a last resort; but now in the key province of
Punjab there was no government to which authority
could be transferred; nor was there the faintest hope that
one might emerge. The lull in Punjab had ended: from
10 May had begun what some observers had described as
a communal war of succession. This conflict was totally
different from the anti-British disturbances of 1942 whose
possible recrudescence in UP and Bihar had been such a
worry to Wavell. Far from defying the police and the
army, the Punjab communal fighters avoided encounters
with the security forces and concentrated upon burning,

stabbing and bomb-throwing—almost impossible to suppress. This, then, was the background to Mountbatten's return. Unless agreement could be arranged, the only alternative was to carry out some kind of partition award under conditions not far from war, or civil war.

Mountbatten's chosen technique was to present his Deal, and to press ahead with such speed that the opposing parties would have no time to develop their own tactics, but would be wholly engaged in keeping up with the working out of the Deal.

The parties agree

Between Mountbatten's return, and his meeting with the leaders on 2 June (as had been announced), only a Saturday and Sunday intervened. At 11 a.m. on the Monday there gathered at Viceroy's House Nehru, Patel, and J. B. Kripalani, representing Congress, Jinnah, Liaqat Ali, and Abdur Rab Nishtar for the League, with Baldev Singh, the Sikh. The meeting lasted two hours, with the Viceroy leading the discussion from beginning to end. First, he announced that he had told the British government that the Muslim League would not withdraw its objections to the Cabinet Mission Scheme. Jinnah nodded his agreement, and they passed quickly on to the new Deal.

And so, by a nod, the Scheme which had been conceived by the ingenuity of one of the greatest of legal brains, which had occupied the attentions of statesmen and politicians, which had been rejected, disputed, and then accepted by the Congress, was finally abandoned.

The draft of the Deal which was to be announced as a statement by the British government was handed to the leaders. They were asked to give the replies of the organizations they represented by midnight. Jinnah protested against the division of Punjab and Bengal, but admitted that he was hopeful of obtaining the agreement of his

Council when it met on 10 June. Now Jinnah's attitude
to commitments was meticulously clear: if he said 'maybe',
then he might go into reverse, but if he said 'yes', then he
would stick scrupulously to his word. Mountbatten knew
his man, and he asked whether the British Prime Minister
should go ahead with his statement? Jinnah said 'yes'; and
that secured the agreement of the League. The agreement
of Congress and the Akali Dal (the Sikh organization)
was given by letter.

Another meeting took place next day. The Viceroy
began by observing that the Deal 'represented as near
100 per cent agreement as it was possible to get' and his
visitors assented. There were some small attempts at
bargaining. Nehru asked that the NWFP referendum
might include as one of the options the choice of independence. Mountbatten countered with a reminder of Nehru's
indignation over 'Balkanization'.[2] By such interjections
the Viceroy was able to avoid direct disputation between
the party leaders. To bring the meeting down from the
clouds of party polemic to the dusty realities of government, Mountbatten now produced a long paper prepared
by his secretariat, *The Administrative Consequences of Partition*.
As they turned over the 34 closely typed pages with their
columns of detail, the startled politicians were at last
brought face to face with the significance of their
wheeling and dealing in practical decision-making.

As soon as the acceptance of the Indian leaders was
confirmed, the Prime Minister informed the House of
Commons on 3 June of the details of Mountbatten's Deal.[3]
The statement began by registering the fact that eight
provinces (Madras, Bombay, United Provinces, Central
Provinces, Bihar, Orissa, Assam, North-West Frontier

[2] Although Congress withdrew its claim for independence for the Frontier,
Nehru gave the movement for Pakhtoonistan his verbal support in later
years.

[3] *Indian Policy: Statement of 3rd June*, 1947, Cmd. 7136.

Province) were already participating, as regards the majority of their elected representatives, in the Constituent Assembly formed under the terms of the Cabinet Mission Scheme. However, the Muslim League was not taking part in the Assembly. Failing agreement, the British government was faced with 'the task of devising a method by which the wishes of the Indian people can be ascertained' concerning the future. The British government intended to leave the issue to India: 'Nor is there anything in this plan to preclude negotiations between communities for a united India'.

The choice: India or Pakistan

The areas where a substantial degree of non-co-operation in the existing Constituent Assembly had been manifested would be asked to decide whether they wanted a future constitution to be framed by the existing assembly or by a 'new and separate Constituent Assembly'. The procedure to be employed was as follows:

Bengal and the Punjab: the provincial legislatures were to meet in two parts, one representing the Muslim-majority districts, the other the remainder; the two parts were to be asked to vote whether or not the province should be partitioned; a simple majority in favour in either part would decide the issue for partition. If the demand was made, the assembly might have a preliminary joint meeting in which a vote would be taken on whether, if the province remained united, it should adhere to the existing Constituent Assembly, or to a new assembly.

North-West Frontier Province: a referendum; in which the electorate for the provincial assembly could vote.

British Baluchistan: no procedure indicated; the Viceroy would ascertain 'how this can most appropriately be done' (actually, as we have noted, by Quetta municipality and tribal representatives).

Assam: if Bengal decided for partition, then a referendum would be held in the Muslim-majority district of Sylhet.

The voting on partition was on a basis of Muslim-majority districts and others. But this was too arbitrary a basis for the actual determination of the line of partition. A Boundary Commission would be appointed to demarcate actual boundaries.

A further section was headed 'Necessity for Speed', and began: 'In order that the successor authorities may have time to prepare themselves to take over power . . .'. This led on to a section headed 'Immediate transfer of power', which indicated that the British government was prepared to hand over 'at an even earlier date' than June 1948. The statement went on:

Accordingly, as the most expeditious, and indeed the only practicable, way of meeting this desire [for an early transfer] His Majesty's Government propose to introduce legislation during the current session for the transfer of power this year on a Dominion status basis to one or two successor authorities according to the decisions taken as a result of this announcement. . . .

In India, the statement was given to the people by radio broadcasts delivered on the evening of 3 June by the Viceroy, Nehru, Jinnah, and Baldev Singh. The next day, Mountbatten faced an audience of 300 reporters in a 'free for all' press conference. Among the hundred questions which were asked, a number probed into the fate of the Sikhs in Punjab: the 'notional' boundary which emerged from the classification of Muslim- and non-Muslim-majority districts clearly placed a large part of the Sikh community within the Pakistan sector. Mountbatten expressed concern, but added little or nothing to the previous day's statement where, in the course of twenty-one detailed paragraphs, the name 'Sikh' was nowhere mentioned. Another question about the timetable for the transfer of power elucidated the reply that this 'could be about the 15th of August'.

Accelerating independence

The question as to exactly when and why a date for handing over power at such short notice was decided, is one to which this essay cannot supply an answer. It appears that during Mountbatten's ten-day London visit, the date of transfer was provisionally agreed for some time towards the end of 1947: already six months in advance of the date set in the announcement of 20 February. In the early drafts of the Bill to make provision for the transfer of power 'the appointed day' seems to have been envisaged as 1 October 1947. Yet within a few days of the press conference (4 June) the terminal date of 15 August had become generally known and accepted.[4] Speaking in the Constituent Assembly in 1949, Sardar Patel asserted that the price Congress had demanded for agreeing to partition was first, that Britain should withdraw from India within two months, and second, that Britain would give Congress a free hand in settling the future of the princely states.[5] This claim has

[4] Though it appears that on 10 June Nehru was still under the impression that the final transfer of power would take place in June 1948 (see Campbell-Johnson, pp. 116–17).

[5] Const. Ass. Deb., vol. 10, no. 3, p. 49, 10 Oct. 1949:

Sardar Patel: 'I give you this inner history which nobody knows. I agreed to partition as a last resort, when we had reached a stage where we could have lost all. . . . At that stage we agreed to partition . . . on the terms that the Punjab should be partitioned—they [the Muslim League] wanted the whole of it—that Bengal should be partitioned—they wanted Calcutta and the whole of it. . . . I made a further condition that in two months' time power should be transferred and an Act should be passed by Parliament in that time, if it was guaranteed that the British government would not interfere with the question of the Indian States. We said "We will deal with that question. . . . The Princes are ours, and we shall deal with them". On those conditions the Bill in Parliament was passed in two months, agreed to by all the three parties. Show me any instance in the history of the British Parliament when such a Bill was passed in two months. But this was done.'

never (within my knowledge) been repeated by any other Indian leader: nor did this somewhat sensational revelation by Patel arouse comment at the time. It was Mountbatten's custom to subject every important issue to what Americans inelegantly but effectively describe as a 'bull-session' among his personal staff. Detailed records of these searching examinations of the issues were minuted. It is said that the decision to advance the date of transfer was evolved by this method of corporate discussion and conclusion.

It may be that the decision (so momentous in retrospect) did not appear controversial at the time to the participants. One year later, Mountbatten was to comment:

Everybody wanted the greatest possible speed, everybody wanted the transfer of power to take place quickly. Indeed, why wait? For in waiting there would be the risk of continued and increasing riots. . . . So we went ahead and fixed a date. It took two years to separate Sind from Bombay. We separated four hundred million people in two-and-a-half months.[6]

The Viceroy's technique of negotiation by acceleration succeeded in carrying the two major protagonists, Congress and the League, along with him. Immediately after the announcement and the press conference, it appeared as if Gandhi might try to reverse the Deal. On 5 June Mountbatten went to see Gandhi, and found him very depressed. The Viceroy told the Mahatma that the so-called Mountbatten Plan was the Gandhi Plan, because all the salient ingredients—such as leaving the choice of their future to the Indian people themselves, avoiding coercion, and transferring power as soon as possible—had been taken from him.[7] Reassured by the Viceroy, Gandhi went on to announce publicly:

The British Government is not responsible for partition.

[6] *Address to East India Ass.*, 29 June 1948.
[7] Campbell-Johnson, p. 110.

The Viceroy has no hand in it. In fact, he is as opposed to division as Congress itself. But if both of us, Hindus and Muslims, cannot agree on anything else, then the Viceroy is left with no choice.

Congress and the League choose

The Council of the Muslim League considered the Deal on 10 June. With 400 voting in the affirmative, and 8 against, they passed a resolution saying that though they could not agree to the partition of Bengal and Punjab, in considering the proposals as a whole they authorized Jinnah to accept the 3 June Deal as a 'compromise'. This guarded endorsement aroused the suspicions of Nehru and Patel, who demanded a firm acceptance. When this was put to Liaqat Ali he replied that after the League had accepted the Cabinet Mission Scheme, Congress had put such reservations on its later 'acceptance' that the League had been compelled to withdraw their consent. They would not be out-manoeuvred again. A possible compromise was suggested in a joint declaration by Jinnah as President of the League and Kripalani as Congress President: this did not come off, though the whole question of formal acceptance became academic when the immutable process of preparation for the transfer gathered way.

The All-India Congress Committee met to consider the Deal on 14 June. A resolution was moved affirming the faith of the Congress in the unity of India (Jinnah did not bother to cavil at this) while accepting the proposals of 3 June. The resolution was moved by Pandit Pant, Premier of the UP, and one of the stalwarts in Patel's camp. The Sardar supported acceptance in unemotional tones. Opposition came mainly from two widely separated groups: the Nationalist Muslims, who felt that Congress was betraying everything they had sacrificed to uphold, and the orthodox Hindus, such as Purshottamdas Tandon, who saw the Deal as abject surrender to the British and the Muslims. Gandhi put his influence behind the resolution, which was passed by 157 votes to 29, with 32 abstentions.

The provinces choose

The meetings of the provincial legislatures to vote upon their constitutional future may be considered here, as the final acts which confirmed the choice for partition.

The Bengal legislature met on 20 June. A request for a preliminary joint meeting was made, and so both parts of the province voted together on the question of a United Bengal adhering to the existing Constituent Assembly or joining a new (Pakistan) assembly. The voting was in favour of joining a new assembly: 126 to 90 votes. Then, in separate meetings, East Bengal endorsed the vote for a united province by 106 to 35, and by 105 to 34 declared in favour of joining a new assembly, i.e. Pakistan. West Bengal decided by 58 to 21 votes for partition, and adhering to the existing Constituent Assembly. By the decision of the West Bengal representatives, Mother Bengal, the land of poets and revolutionaries, was to be divided.

The Punjab legislature met on 23 June. At a preliminary meeting both parts of the assembly voted together on the question of adhering to the existing Constituent Assembly or to a new assembly. By 91 votes to 77, the joint body voted in favour of a new assembly, or Pakistan. Then a separate meeting of the representatives of East Punjab voted 50 to 27 for partition and adhering to the existing Constituent Assembly. The Western representatives declared for Pakistan and no partition by 69 to 27 votes. The decision by East Punjab for partition prevailed: the Land of the Five Rivers was now only a geographical expression.

The Sind legislature met on 26 June, and by 33 votes to 20 decided for Pakistan.

In Baluchistan, 54 members of Quetta municipality voted for Pakistan, with 3 members absent. Spokesmen of the *Shahi Jirga* also chose Pakistan.

A referendum was staged in Sylhet on 6 and 7 July. An intensive propaganda campaign was mounted by Congress and the League: neither side was assured of victory. At the count, 239,619 persons voted for separation from Assam and union with the new East Bengal, while 184,041 voted against.

On the Frontier, the referendum was carried out under a new Governor, General Sir Rob Lockhart, after Congress had alleged that the previous Governor favoured the League. Pashtu-speaking British officers of the Indian army were imported as impartial umpires to supervise the polling. The Red Shirt leader, Khan Abdul Ghaffar Khan, instructed his followers to boycott the poll as they were not allowed to vote for a separate Pakhtoonistan. Of the registered electors (572,798) about 49 per cent (280,680) did not vote; 2,874 voted to stay with India, and 289,244 voted for Pakistan. Thus some 51 per cent of the *total* electorate voted for Pakistan—despite the boycott—and gave their verdict upon Nehru's claim that the Frontier was a Congress province.[8]

And so Mountbatten carried through his intention to devise a Deal whereby the peoples of India could determine their own future. They had made their decision. But the burden of implementing the Deal, of setting up the machinery to convert a paper plan into reality remained;

[8] Old legends die slowly. Many in India still believe that if the Red Shirts had not boycotted the referendum the vote would have gone against Pakistan. Khan Abdul Ghaffar Khan knew well that to urge his followers to vote for India would be to commit political suicide, whereas Pathan separatism was a popular platform. Yet Sri Prakasa, the first High Commissioner for India at Karachi, writes in his *Pakistan; Birth and Early Days* (Meerut, 1965), p. 131: 'His vote and the votes of his Red Shirts and other followers might have turned the balance; but as those who do not vote lose their votes, the majority of votes cast went in favour of Pakistan.'

to be discharged by the Viceroy, his Council, and hundreds of others, Indian and British, in Delhi and London. From the publication of the Deal to the transfer of power there were seventy days in which to complete a thousand necessary tasks.

8

Implementing the Deal
(June–August 1947)

At about this time, a senior British civil servant noted:

We are now transferring power; anything that does happen in India will happen because the Indians agree to it or acquiesce in it. Our only assets are the force of habit (a big one), the probability that much administrative machinery will run on because nobody has time to stop it or knows that it is running on, and the personality of the Viceroy and some of the Governors.

Once 3 June was passed, although in form there were opportunities for halting the march towards partition, in actuality the Rubicon had been crossed, and all that remained was to work out the implications of the choice: as Mountbatten emphasized so powerfully when he produced, at the 3 June meeting at Viceroy's House, the shattering document *The Administrative Consequences of Partition* for the leaders to study and implement. At this hour, British statesmen and administrators might well have said 'We have done our part: now it is up to you', and sat back to watch the Congress and League leadership begin the novel experience of actually taking the responsibility for the consequences of their words. In fact, during the last six or seven weeks of the Raj, the erstwhile rulers made their last and greatest effort to hand over a functioning political system to their successors.

The actual conduct of the interim government was in the hands of a team of ministers whom Mountbatten treated as a Cabinet, but who showed not the slightest sense of collective responsibility. In some of the departments, the political heads exercised no real control, being preoccupied with politics. By contrast, other ministers firmly applied themselves to the work of governing. Sardar Patel was consolidating his position at the centre of the web of administration, singling out the Indian officials he could trust to take on the new responsibilities. He was taking the hard decisions without reference to his Congress colleagues. As one example: it was virtually certain that Calcutta would fall to Hindustan, but most of the hinterland would go to Pakistan. It was suggested that if Pakistan had access to Calcutta's facilities, concessions might be extracted in exchange, which would lessen the barriers of partition. An emissary was sent to Patel, to propose that Calcutta should be placed under joint control for six months. With notable economy of words, the Sardar dismissed the project: 'Not even for six hours'.

The interim government divides

There were not so many examples of tough decision-making. More typical was a 'Cabinet' meeting on 8 June, which Mountbatten opened by proposing that, in view of the short time before independence, no major new appointments should be initiated meanwhile. This proposal was accepted. Thereupon, Nehru announced a list of new diplomatic appointments. Liaqat Ali interjected that he could not see the need for some of these: for example, he did not want an ambassador at Moscow. As Nehru's sister, Mrs Pandit, was about to be nominated for this post, this precipitated a scene. Nehru announced that he would not tolerate interference by the Muslim League in the affairs of the government. He would insist on these matters being put to a vote, and he would ensure that the League was outvoted every time. Everyone talked at once, and quiet was only restored by the Viceroy calling each member present to order by name.[1]

Throughout June the Congress pressed for the government to be split into two parts. In response to these pleas, Mountbatten suggested to Jinnah that the 'Cabinet' might be divided into two committees, each member taking two portfolios, the League members holding the 'Pakistan' portfolios. Jinnah declined, and pointed out that this procedure would not be permissible under the Government of India Act from which their authority derived. Nehru pressed the matter to the point of issuing an ultimatum at the end of June; but when the matter was referred to London, there was a prompt rejection. When the legislation for partition came into force on 18 July Mountbatten promptly issued an order (as he was now empowered to do) placing the affairs of Hindustan under the Congress ministers and those of Pakistan under the League. The last meeting of the full interim government took place on 16 July. Thereafter there were joint meetings of the two parts under the Viceroy to discuss common subjects: but in general the two halves of the Council functioned as two rival governments.

Choosing heads of state

A good deal of attention was devoted during June to the question of the post of Governor-General under the new regime. Mountbatten rigorously dissociated himself from the most contentious aspects of partition—the division of the assets, material and financial, throughout the sub-continent, and the determination of the boundary

[1] Campbell-Johnson, p. 114.

lines between the new states. But he appears to have absorbed something of the 'umpire' concept which Gandhi and Nehru had so often proposed: and so he conceived the idea that he might become joint Governor-General of both the new Dominions, having already received a cordial invitation from Nehru and Congress to be their Governor-General. Such an idea was certainly no more esoteric than the prevailing concept of the British monarch as the ruler of the individual Dominions of the Commonwealth. It would have immense practical advantages in providing a measure of continuity and association for the two newly-divided states. During the early stages of drafting the legislation which was to give the new states their legal personality, the assumption was made that the new Governor-General would hold dual office. When this proposition was put to Jinnah, he countered with the suggestion that Hindustan and Pakistan should each have a separate Governor-General, but that Mountbatten should become a super Governor-General, a supreme co-ordinator. This introduced a constitutional concept of such oddity that even the British Commonwealth had no place for it: the proposal for a dual Governor-General was therefore renewed. No reply could be obtained, until at last, on 2 July, Jinnah indicated that he would become the first Governor-General of Pakistan. He explained that as all Governors of provinces, save only one, and all the heads of the armed services were to be British, it was essential that the Governor-General should be a Pakistani. Even this announcement was not taken as final. A suggestion was made that Jinnah might be content to function as 'officiating Governor-General', while Mountbatten as titular Governor-General held a watching brief for Pakistan in Delhi. Not unnaturally, this was not acceptable. These exchanges chilled the relations between Mountbatten and Jinnah, and made it difficult for the Viceroy to feel the same enthusiasm for Pakistan which he entertained towards the new India.[2]

The Sikhs in limbo

If Mountbatten's almost instinctive touch in dealing with Asian peoples was deficient in his dealings with the Muslim leaders, it was also lacking in his connexions with the Sikhs. One of the reasons why Mountbatten's negotiations with Congress and the League had ended in an agreed Deal was that there had been an identifiable party with whom to negotiate. The Muslims of India had (except for an isolated minority) taken Jinnah, *Qaid-i-Azam*, the 'Great Leader', as their spokesman, and followed his decisions. For the remaining peoples of India, there was the Congress; a cohesive organization, with its lines of communication extending throughout the provinces and districts. The Congress leadership had maintained a united front during the last long year; and even if some to Left or Right might dissent, there was the central organization, with its established rules and procedure, to see the Deal through. But the Sikhs acknowledged no inspired leader and no central organization. It had always been so; the secret strength of the Sikhs in the days of persecution was their loose association in *misls* or clans which could disperse or unite as the occasion demanded. Out of the array of Sikh politicians, Baldev Singh had been singled out to act as the Sikh spokesman. Not only was he unable to 'deliver' the support of the Sikhs: he had not been able to obtain anything from the British government in the way of concessions to 'deliver' to his people. He was a middleman in the middle of a vacuum. If the Sikhs had found

[2] This is an appropriate place in the text to abandon the use of the term 'Hindustan' which the Congress had signified was objectionable for a secular state. Moreover the fundamental reason why people such as Nehru could swallow partition was the deeply-held belief that the continuity of India had been preserved.

themselves in the Group B of the Cabinet Mission's Scheme, they would have been able to wring concessions from the Muslim-majority community. Straddled across the future line of partition in the Punjab, they could not expect to exercise any significant influence, by reason of their numbers alone, in either of the new Dominions. However, at the prompting of individual British sympathizers, such as Penderel Moon, Giani Kartar Singh (one of the principals in the claim for Khalistan) endeavoured to obtain some recognition for the Sikhs' claim to nationhood within Pakistan.[3] It seems that they asked for the status of a 'sub-nation' with the right of secession. Jinnah showed no disposition to make concessions to the Sikhs. As we have seen, his attitude had changed, and from viewing Pakistan as an extended polity in which the Muslim would be *primus inter pares* he had settled for a narrower Pakistan in which the Muslim would be master.

And so the moment for Muslim–Sikh negotiation passed. The Sikhs were not dismayed. They knew that their skill lay not in words but in deeds. The alert went out from one Sikh settlement to the next; they sharpened their swords and waited. Mountbatten received due warning of these developments. Some of his advisers urged that he should anticipate trouble and take the ring-leaders into custody. But there were some who retorted that if all the potential trouble-makers were to be put behind bars there would be no one in Punjab to whom the British could hand over at the appointed day. Mountbatten held his hand: besides, he reckoned that he had the answer to trouble in a special military *corps d'elite*, the Punjab Boundary Force.

Dividing an army

The Indian army was obviously a key factor, if not the key factor, in the successful realization of the Deal. Ever

[3] Penderel Moon, *Divide and Quit* (1961), pp. 82–87.

since the Mutiny, ninety years before, it had been basic policy to introduce into almost every regiment and corps a calculated balance between the 'martial races' of India. This meant that—apart from the Gurkha and Garhwali battalions, which enlisted only one linguistic and religious type—all formations (including most of the ancillary services) were made up of 'class' companies or squadrons. Infantry battalions might be known as the 'Sikhs' or the 'Rajputs', and yet include companies of Punjabi Muslims.[4] This communal composition had been compatible with a tremendous regimental spirit and genuine comradeship between the different 'races'. Some said that the Indian army was the only genuine non-communal institution in India: and this was the force which must also be arbitrarily partitioned, like the country. One senior officer, General Tuker, had submitted a plan at the end of 1945 for the regrouping of units throughout the army into Muslim, Hindu, and Sikh elements. Tuker's plan was put aside during Wavell's tenure of office. To have regrouped the army into Muslim, Hindu, and Sikh units would have gone a long way to accept the assumption that Pakistan was inevitable: which, of course, was the direct antithesis of Wavell's policy. When Mountbatten first arrived in India he tackled Field-Marshal Auchinleck, the Commander-in-Chief, on the subject, and was told that the division of the army on communal lines would take from five to ten years. Auchinleck had been a Punjabi infantryman, and he knew well the close comradeship between Punjabi Muslim, Sikh, and Hindu within the family of the regiment. As the crazy hatred between the communities was being enlarged, like a cancerous growth on the life of India, Auchinleck regarded the Indian army's

---

[4] In the British army, battalions of the Scots Guards often have an Irish contingent, the 'Mick Company'. But this is because it is easier to find Irish than Scottish recruits; it is not deliberate policy, as in the old Indian army.

tradition of solidarity as the last bastion between order and chaos.

At first, Mountbatten accepted the position. On 8 April, after representations by Liaqat Ali on the need for re-organization, the Viceroy laid down that there would be no splitting of the army before the British withdrew: 'The mechanics won't permit it, and I won't'.[5] Everything changed when the Deal was accepted, and Mountbatten began to consider partition of the armed forces. However, Auchinleck still could not reconcile himself to being the instrument of the dismemberment of the old Indian army, and not until early July was a firm decision taken. It was agreed that the new Dominions must be able to call upon a command structure and upon certain operational units when 15 August came. At this time Muslims comprised about 36 or 37 per cent of the strength, according to the Armed Forces Reconstitution Committee, but the question was whether apportionment to Pakistan or the new India should be on a basis of religion or of domicile. A high proportion of the fighting troops were Punjabis: what of the Sikh who found his home-place within the boundary of Pakistan? No complete formula was laid down, but in general for a volunteer army the principle of choice would prevail.

It was agreed to constitute a Joint Defence Council, composed of the Governor-General and Defence Minister of each Dominion, with Auchinleck as Supreme Commander. An armed forces reconstruction committee was also agreed upon; the target date for the final 'reconstruction' of the forces was envisaged as 1 April 1948. Another question for decision by the political leaders was the future role of British forces in India. When the former 'white' colonies of the British Empire had acquired self-government, they had accepted (many had welcomed) the

[5] Campbell-Johnson, p. 58.

continuing presence of British military and naval units for a further period. Even Eire had accepted the continuation of British naval stations on her coasts for seventeen years after the Anglo-Irish Treaty of 1921. The departure of the British troops had been the principal feature of the Quit India campaign, and almost all pronouncements by Gandhi and Nehru. By contrast, Jinnah regarded the continuing presence of British forces as a safeguard; while British military planners continually emphasized that Pakistan on her own could not maintain watch and ward on the North-West Frontier. Already there had been a substantial run-down of British troops since 1945. Less than half the number of British infantry battalions maintained in the normal Indian establishment remained. It was agreed, as a compromise between the viewpoints of Nehru and Jinnah, to withdraw all British forces within six months of independence. During the interim period they would not be used in an operational role.[6]

Policing an unmade frontier

The deteriorating situation in Punjab was drawn to the Viceroy's notice by the Governor, Sir Evan Jenkins, and on 22 July a meeting was arranged with Congress, the League, and Baldev Singh. The leaders issued a joint statement which (in the enthusiasm of the moment) was called a 'charter of rights' for the minorities after partition. The statement also announced the formation of a special Punjab Boundary Force to cover twelve civil districts in Punjab: the whole province, except for the western, south-eastern, and Himalayan extremities. The nucleus of the force was the crack 4th Indian Division, augmented by special units to increase its mobility and communica-

[6] Leonard Mosley's *The Last Days of the British Raj* includes a number of former Top Secret documents, and other confidential material on the role of the British troops, and aspects of partitioning the Indian army (see pp. 137-49).

tions. The commander of the force, Major-General Rees, would be responsible to the Supreme Commander and the Joint Defence Council. The force contained a high proportion of British officers.

When the GOC Eastern Command, General Tuker, was asked whether he wanted a similar boundary force, he declined. Tuker expected (correctly) that trouble would be concentrated in Calcutta which he assumed (correctly) would fall well inside the boundary of the new India. He confined his preparations to placing battalions designated for Pakistan in the heart of the Muslim-majority areas. Tuker was also responsible for the Gangetic plains, and he organized a *cordon sanitaire* to seal off the Punjab with its warring communities from the approaches to the United Provinces.

At the end of July a provisional formula was reached for dividing the defence forces. Of the Indian army, 70 per cent would go to the new India, and 30 per cent to Pakistan. The Royal Indian Navy would be similarly apportioned, 70/30, though 40 per cent of the sailors were Muslims. By contrast, the Indian Air Force was 20 per cent Muslim and 80 per cent non-Muslim. The Congress claimed 8 of the 10 squadrons of the IAF. Mountbatten tried to solve the difficulty by asking for priority to be given to raising an additional Fighter Squadron for Pakistan. The actual posting of personnel to India or Pakistan was in most cases delayed until after partition. Even amid the communal madness of those days, a Muslim company or squadron would be given an affectionate farewell party by their Sikh comrades, or vice versa, with assurances of undying *bhaibandi* or brotherhood. Something of this spirit endured through the long confrontation in Kashmir, and even through the war of September 1965. Communalism *within* the army was mainly confined to the junior officers, though in relation to the world of the civilian the sepoy could be as communally-minded as anyone.

Dividing the assets

There were many issues wider than those of defence which had to be tackled in the light of partition. Immediately the Deal was agreed upon, Mountbatten proposed the setting up of a Partition Committee, over which he would preside, with two representatives from Congress and the League. Those nominated were Patel and Rajendra Prasad, with Liaqat Ali and Nishtar. The Partition Committee met on 13 June, and agreed to appoint a Steering Committee, so-called, comprising two senior civil servants, H. M. Patel (no relation to the Sardar), and Choudhri Mohammad Ali. These two officials were able to set about their task on a professional basis of mutual respect and trust (so alien to the politicians). Only matters in which they could not agree were referred to the Partition Committee proper, and good progress was made in apportioning assets and debits. When Bengal and Punjab had actually voted for partition, the Partition Committee was replaced by a Partition Council (27 June) in which Jinnah took the place of Nishtar. In addition, subordinate bodies were constituted—the Bengal Separation Council, the Punjab Partition Committee, and the Assam Separation Council—to deal with provincial subjects. In the final stage before independence, the Partition Council became virtually the only forum in which there was inter-communication between Congress and League. It met for the last time on August 6.

The machinery of partition

The most vexed question of all was, of course, the line of partition between the two new Dominions. While

Congress had conceded the right of the League and the Muslim-majority areas to go their own way, this was conceded in a spirit of bitter resentment, and there was a determination that they should take with them as little as possible. Jinnah and the League had accepted that the full six-province Pakistan was not attainable, or even desirable: but they still intended to secure a viable Pakistan, where they could be safe and prosper. There was a gulf between these two rival views on partition: and in addition there were the Sikhs, determined to fight for their survival. We have seen that the Sikhs received no place on the Partition Committee or the Partition Council. They had little part in devising the machinery of the Boundary Commission, which was settled between Nehru and Jinnah. The latter favoured inviting the United Nations to adjudicate. One proposal was for a three-man UN Commission with three assessors from each side (India and Pakistan). Another suggestion was for a single arbitrator, perhaps from the UN or the International Court at The Hague. However, Nehru wanted the matter to be settled by Indians, and he proposed a judicial tribunal, with two members nominated by Congress, two by the League, and an independent chairman. Jinnah jibbed at this, remarking 'There was always trouble when two or more lawyers got together', but in the end, because of the need for speed, this procedure was accepted: except that there would be two tribunals, one for Punjab, and one for Bengal and Sylhet. At a meeting of the Partition Council on 13 June, this was agreed, and also the terms of reference which should be employed:

The Boundary Commission is instructed to demarcate the boundaries of the two parts of the Punjab/Bengal on the basis of ascertaining the contiguous majority areas of Muslims and non-Muslims. In doing so, it will also take into account other factors.

What could be more simple: or more vague?

There followed an interval of two weeks, when the names of members of the two commissions were announced. The four members of the Punjab Commission were all members of the Lahore High Court: two Muslims, a Hindu, and a Sikh. The members of the Bengal Commission included two Hindu judges of the Calcutta High Court; a Muslim acting judge of the same court, and a Muslim District and Sessions judge from Punjab. Whereas the Muslim members of the Punjab Commission were just as formidable as their non-Muslim colleagues, the same was hardly true for Bengal. The announcement of a chairman followed next day. The choice was made, after some difficulty, by Nehru and Jinnah, with Mountbatten at their elbow. They agreed upon Sir Cyril Radcliffe, an eminent English Counsel. Agreement on his name was aided by his having had no connexion, however remote, with Indian affairs. It appears that, in inviting him to serve, the British government indicated that his appointment might last for a number of months: in fact, Radcliffe was to spend less than forty days in India. Before leaving London he had an interview with the Prime Minister in which India was not one of the topics discussed. He arrived in Delhi on 8 July, and seems to have sensed very rapidly that his was to be no ordinary chairman's task for, on or by 10 July, he had suggested that the independence Bill which would give legality to the decision of the Boundary Commissions should be modified to include the condition (clauses 3 and 4) that 'the expression "award" means, in relation to a boundary commission, the decisions of the chairman of that commission contained in his report to the Governor-General at the conclusion of the commission's proceedings'.

The partition machinery at work

Because the commissions had been constituted as judicial bodies, they sat as a court and took evidence in much the same manner as in a trial. The hearings took place in Calcutta and Lahore, over 1,000 miles apart, and Radcliffe decided that he could not personally sit with the commissions. He therefore made his head-quarters at Delhi, receiving the transcripts of the hearings every day. The Bengal Commission sat from 16 to 24 July, and then sat again from 4 to 6 August to consider Sylhet. The Punjab Commission sat from 21 to 31 July. The main evidence was presented by Congress and the League, but the Punjab Commission also heard from the Sikhs, the Ahmadiyya, and others. The Bengal Commission heard evidence from the Hindu Mahasabha, the New Bengal Association, and others. There was a good deal of emphasis upon the 'other factors' mentioned in the terms of reference. A somewhat unguarded statement in the House of Commons by Arthur Henderson, the Under Secretary of State, that these 'other factors' could mean, in Punjab, consideration for the Sikh holy places (some of which, like Hassan Abdal, were deep in the Muslim heartland), led to an outburst from Jinnah and the League: was this a last minute sell-out?

Radcliffe met his colleagues of Bengal in Calcutta, after their first deliberations, then went to Simla to confer with the Punjab Commission, and finally came down to Delhi to discuss Sylhet with the Bengal Commission. It became quite clear that there would be no agreement between the Indian judges. Indeed, over Sylhet, the Muslim judges wanted to interpret their mandate to include incorporating territory from other Assam districts, as the somewhat loose wording of their terms of reference permitted.[7] Radcliffe was left with no alternative but to produce an award by himself. In preparation for his lonely task he had isolated himself in separate quarters in New Delhi seeing hardly anyone except his secretary. Now he approached the leaders of Congress and the League and suggested that, as the difficulties involved in his producing an award which would give any satifaction were so immense, he was ready to hand over the labour to the party leaders for them to solve. Both sides replied that whatever he decided was preferable to any attempt by the politicians to evolve a joint boundary.

Radcliffe discovered that his statistical information and even his maps were sometimes deficient. Even when he had established the relative proportions of different communities in different places, this was only a beginning. His object was not to work out the religious complexities of patterns of settlement, but—ultimately—to draw a line upon a map. The 'notional' division of Bengal under the 3 June announcement left three unconnected non-Muslim pieces of territory outside the Pakistan sector: four districts in the south-west, two sub-Himalayan districts, and a tract on the Burma border. What was Radcliffe supposed to do with these? But these were merely the largest of the examples of the random location of Muslims and non-Muslims which he had somehow to overcome in his lines of partition. The Viceroy had made it clear that the award ought to be ready by 15 August. Radcliffe finally completed all his reports and schedules by 13 August. He destroyed all his preliminary sketches for the boundary: he was convinced that his decision

[7] 'In the event of the referendum in the District of Sylhet resulting in favour of amalgamation with Eastern Bengal, the Boundary Commission will also demarcate the Muslim majority areas of Sylhet District and the contiguous Muslim majority areas of the adjoining districts of Assam.'

(which he knew was imperfect, and likely to please nobody) would only stand the test if it was presented as a firm award. And so Radcliffe gave no explanations and made no apologies: he presented his award to the Viceroy, and he departed immediately for London.

Parliament legislates

While these different events were taking place almost simultaneously in India, the legal framework for the transfer of power was being constructed at Westminster. The Government of India Act of 1935 had only become law after two years' debate: first within the Conservative Party and a Joint Select Committee of both Houses of Parliament (April 1933–November 1934) and then for eight months on the floor of the House of Commons, while Winston Churchill and his associates fought a long rearguard action to delay the advance of self-government in India. The parliamentary debates after the Prime Minister's announcement of 20 February had demonstrated that, while the old Churchillian spirit remained, there was little if any support for his stand in the ranks of the Conservatives. During his brief London visit in May, Mountbatten had not neglected to talk to the opposition leaders, and he had convinced them that this was the last chance of agreement in the sub-continent. The Labour government were therefore assured of a smooth passage for their enabling legislation: but even given parliamentary co-operation, it would be a close-run thing.

One great advantage of the acceptance of Dominion status as the vehicle whereby India and Pakistan would travel to independence was that the 1935 Act, somewhat amended, could be utilized as an interim constitution for the new states. The Act had been envisaged as a stepping-stone to self-government by its makers, and now it was to serve the new states well: indeed, with some further modification, the 1935 Act provided Pakistan with its constitution for nine years after independence! When the Lord Chancellor and the Law Officers were first consulted in May, they advised that a non-contro-versial Bill could be prepared within six weeks of a definite decision as to what was required. In the event, they completed the necessary legislation within four weeks. Many new provisions (such as that relating to the award of the chairman of the Boundary Commission) had to be inserted in the light of changing events. Drafts were referred to Mountbatten, and he exercised his influence on matters of policy. One consideration was the future of the dependencies of the sub-continent, in particular, the Andaman and Nicobar Islands. During a century and a half of British rule, control from India had radiated out over the whole Indian Ocean area. Some of these outer dependencies had been separated from India long before, like Singapore in 1867. Others had been separated more recently—like Aden—transferred to Colonial Office control in 1937. There was a good case for treating the Andamans as having no organic relation with the sub-continent, and retaining them under British rule as potentially useful strategic outposts. Proposals from the defence side on these lines were resisted by the Viceroy and overruled by the Prime Minister. Similarly, when a clause was inserted into the draft Bill to provide the Governor-General with certain powers to override the ministers, *after* independence, in respect of matters relating to disputes between the new Dominions, Mountbatten refused to consider such a proposal. Instead, a special Arbitral Tribunal was set up to deal with inter-Dominion disputes.

Independence made complete

The great experiment which was initiated in this transfer of power to India and Pakistan was independence without strings of any sort. When, in the previous year, the Philippines had obtained their independence from the United States, the termination of American rule was accompanied by a series of agreements which gave the Americans access to a protected market, military bases in perpetuity, and other concessions which secured for the United States an outpost in South East Asia. When France and the Netherlands came to consider the process of decolonization a few years later, they also attempted to bind the newly independent former colonies by ties of various kinds. The evolution of the 'white' Dominions had also been accompanied by a gradual severing of the links between the Mother Country and her children. But in August 1947, India and Pakistan became genuinely independent: and no effort was made by Britain to set a limit to this independence.

The transformation was symbolized by the title of the Bill which brought this about: the Indian Independence Bill. There were some in the opposition who thought that this title was unnecessarily sweeping; why not the Indian Dominion Bill? Reference was made to the Dominion Prime Ministers. Strangely enough, the leaders of the two countries which had made most of severing United Kingdom control over the Commonwealth, Smuts of South Africa and Mackenzie King of Canada, were least enthusiastic about the term 'independence'. But no change was made in the title.

At the beginning of July, when the Bill was ready for submission to parliament, as a gesture of goodwill its contents were shown to Nehru and Jinnah. The two leaders scrutinized the measure for some hours. True to form, Nehru compiled a long list of the amendments he desired to be incorporated—mainly designed to emphasize that Pakistan was an artificial creation, whereas the new India was the continuing body of the sub-continent. His

amendments were not included. The Bill was first introduced in the House of Commons on 4 July. It passed its
third reading through both Houses on 15 July, and came
into force on 18 July 1947. The speeches in both Houses
of Parliament were fitting for the occasion, expressing a
sense of a trust fulfilled. It was a little too early for British
statesmen to employ the tones of high achievement. Much
had been done; but this was only the beginning of a long,
hard road to be covered.

The last watch

Perhaps the men who really kept faith in this hour were
the 2,500 British officers of the old Indian army who
volunteered to stay on with the forces of the new India
and Pakistan, and the British members of the Indian Civil
Service who also chose to stay; despite the abuse that had
been poured on their heads by politicians. These men
now prepared to soldier on a little longer until they were
asked to hand over to their Indian and Pakistani successors. As independence day approached, the boundaries
between the two countries that were to emerge were still
not known: the Radcliffe award was not published
(on Mountbatten's instructions) until after 15 August.[8]
In Punjab the districts whose future was most open to
speculation were those of Lahore, Amritsar, and Gurdaspur. In each of these districts a British Deputy Commissioner and a British Superintendent of Police continued
on duty. Their potential replacements stood by—Indian
and Pakistani both—waiting to hear which would be
required. As much in the dark as their successors, the
British officers waited, and watched.

[8] *Gazette of India Extraordinary* (New Delhi), 17 Aug. 1947. Legislative
Department (Reforms): . . . 'The Reports of the Bengal Boundary Commission and of the Punjab Boundary Commission are published for general
information.'

9

Consequences and Causes

THE 15th of August 1947 marks the end of the story which this essay has tried to tell. Up to that day, the India Office was (as described elsewhere)[1] 'the communications centre of the greatest imperial possession on earth'. Suddenly, all was silence. The cables which had poured in every hour, relaying intelligence from every corner of the sub-continent, abruptly ceased. From now on, the British government was only a spectator. Whatever information British diplomatic representatives could glean from senior officials or ministers was passed on; the columns of the newspapers were scanned and filed: and that was that. What the British government or people thought about the sub-continent no longer had any effect.

The partition award

But the consequences of British actions before independence went on having their effects for some time. First came the announcement of the Radcliffe award. On 15 August Mountbatten reminded the Constituent Assembly of India that 'It was they [the Indian leaders] who selected the personnel of the Boundary Commissions, including the chairman; it was they who drew up the terms of reference; it is they who shoulder the responsibility for implementing the award.'[2] This exordium had

[1] Tinker, *Reorientations*, p. 8.
[2] Const. Ass. Deb., vol. 5, no. 2, p. 16.

little immediate effect. Both sides had put in such extravagant claims that they were bound to be disappointed. India had little cause for complaint. As we have seen, Lord Radcliffe studiously declined to reveal the basis on which his award was made: but it appears that he adopted the attitude that it was for the Pakistan leaders to establish a case as to whether they should receive an area, rather than the reverse. In the partition of Bengal, Murshidabad District, the centre of the old Muslim culture and tradition, was allotted to India. Other Muslim-majority districts were divided, and the allocation of Khulna with a thin Hindu majority was not adequate recompense. However, the Chittagong Hill Tracts were given to Pakistan, although not included under the 'notional' distribution of the Indian Independence Act. The Tracts were peopled by tribal peoples, Animists and Buddhists. If they were not Muslim, they were not Hindu either.[3] It may be inferred that the Tracts went to Pakistan because their communications, such as they were, ran down to the Chittagong area, and future development depended upon Chittagong proper and the Tracts being under the same administration. Altogether West Bengal gained substantially over East Bengal under the award.[4] However, this did not prevent a blaze of indignation from the Congress side over the allocation of the Chittagong Hill Tracts. At first it even seemed possible that India would repudiate the award; however, calmer reasoning prevailed in the end. Although East Pakistan had cause to be disappointed, the League

[3] Murshidabad District included 927,747 Muslims and 684,937 non-Muslims, according to the 1941 Census. Khulna District contained 977,693 non-Muslims and 959,172 Muslims. Chittagong Hill Tracts contained a population of 247,000, of whom 233,000 were Buddhists/Animists, 7,000 Muslims, and 7,000 Hindus.

[4] However, as V. P. Menon (p. 402) points out, the Radcliffe award put only 16 per cent. of the Muslims of undivided Bengal into West Bengal (India), whereas 42 per cent. of the non-Muslims found themselves in East Bengal (Pakistan). It would have appeared inequitable to load the balance still further in Pakistan's favour.

leaders protested not at all at the Bengal result. Their indignation was focused upon the allocation of Gurdaspur District to India, though it formed a part of the 'notional' West Punjab under the Indian Independence Act.[5] Far from time healing the feeling of injury, this became even more intense as a result of the Maharaja of Kashmir acceding to India. The main route linking the Indian Union with Kashmir runs through the foothills of Gurdaspur. Pakistanis came to believe that Kashmir could not have been taken by India had Gurdaspur gone to Pakistan.

As a result of this grievance, a myth developed, alleging that Lord Mountbatten intervened to cause the boundary to be altered to Pakistan's disadvantage. Perhaps, in the first place, the postponement of the publication of the award provided the foundation for the legend. Despite these antagonisms, the award was not challenged. Subsequent attempts to rectify some anomalies, especially on the Bengal border, have not given mutual satisfaction, and almost everywhere the border so hastily chalked out by Radcliffe remains, twenty years later, the recognized international frontier between India and Pakistan. In politics the acid test for success is survival. The Radcliffe award has survived two decades of acute tension between these two uneasy neighbours. To have done so, it must have represented a certain rough justice.

Alternatives to the award

Could a better means of frontier delimitation have been devised? The key factor in Radcliffe's situation was time: he had to complete his award within little more than

---

[5] Muslims formed about 55 per cent. of the population of Gurdaspur District (Muslims = 589,923, Sikhs = 221,261, Hindus = 283,192). Muslims were in a clear majority in three of the four *tehsils* (revenue units) of the district, but the Radcliffe award gave Pakistan only the trans-Ravi *tehsil*.

one month. It is in relation to the actual demarcation that the decision to advance the date of the transfer of power looks most questionable. The right course would have been to present a boundary award well ahead of the transfer date, and then to make the necessary adjustments, in the movement of population, if necessary, and in the negotiation of mutual arrangements for access to facilities in the neighbouring country. If independence had been deferred even to 31 December, 1947, and the award had been published on 1 October, 1947, then forward planning would have been possible.

During June and July it was put to the Congress and League leaders that they ought to consider a programme for a transfer of population, so that Muslims, Hindus, and Sikhs might have the opportunity to make their homes in the land of their choice. Both sides refused absolutely to consider any transfer: presumably because they anticipated that any withdrawal of population from an area would concede that area to the other party. If the award had already been published, there would have been no advantage in leaving hostages to fortune, and those who had found themselves a minority could have made a rational choice.

Another questionable feature of the Boundary Commissions was their judicial character. There were established techniques for drawing boundaries where populations were an ethnographic muddle, such as had been applied by the League of Nations in determining certain boundaries of the succession states of the Habsburg Empire. In India, a finely developed instrument for establishing the patterns of habitation existed, immediately available, in the Land Settlement staff, whose surveys have recorded a Domesday Book of rural India, field by field. Given a few months, a special Settlement operation could have been mounted to compile a detailed survey of human and economic patterns in the marginal areas. From these surveys, experts in boundary questions could have constructed a reasonably scientific frontier.

Of course, such an operation would have entailed employing hundreds of officials drawn from district administration, and by mid-1947, the politicians—the Congress especially—were morbidly suspicious of officials. But it should have been possible to create teams led by civil servants whom both sides could trust, and who could trust each other—in the same way that H. M. Patel and Mohammad Ali worked in apportioning assets. One suspects that the lawyer-politicians never realized that such a course was possible.

A frontier in disorder

The second big decision, taken immediately before independence, when put to the test had an unsuccessful outcome. This was the decision to set up the Joint Defence Council and the Punjab Boundary Force. The Boundary Force, in which such faith had been placed, could not prevent a complete breakdown of intercommunal relations in central and eastern Punjab. The story has been told in some detail in Penderel Moon's *Divide and Quit* (pp. 279–81), where the Sikhs emerge as the central impetus in the tidal wave of hatred and murder. The Force found itself quite unable to take effective action when it was blind and deaf to so much that was going on. Soon it found itself a kind of whipping-boy for the inability of higher authority to control events, and within a few weeks it was dispersed: not before it had carried out a great number of operations of rescue and succour.

Some have ascribed the failure of the Boundary Force to hold the situation in balance to the growing communal

spirit in the army. But the reason was much more fundamental: the army was required to act as a substitute for
the police force, and it was neither trained nor equipped
to act as police. Something like the same mistake has been
made in Vietnam, where the decision to counter guerrilla
activities by military, not police, action led inexorably to
an escalation from sabotage to insurrection to war. What
happened in Punjab in the summer of 1947 was a complete
breakdown of communication between authority and the
people. Law and order depends upon information: no
information was reaching the civil power because the
civil police had ceased to function effectively, while the
village headmen and other contacts had withdrawn into
their own local community.[6] Attempts by the Boundary
Force to restore order by punitive measures often exacerbated the tendencies to violence. Meanwhile, the local
political leaders who ought to have been working in the
villages to restore calm and confidence were often taking
the lead in whipping up popular frenzy.

However, the politicians chose to blame the killings
upon the Punjab Boundary Force. From India, came pressure to wind it up. From 1 September its units were
transferred to India and Pakistan. This led directly to the
resignation of the force commander, Major-General Rees,
and indirectly to the premature retirement of Field-
Marshal Auchinleck as Supreme Commander. He was
not replaced, and the Joint Defence Council virtually
ceased to function. It was formally abolished on 1 April
1948. The Arbitral Tribunal also came to an end on

[6] A question which requires further examination concerning the last
years of British rule is the relation of police organization to the main-
tenance of law and order. In the United Provinces, the police had maintained
a high state of efficiency and morale all through the trouble of 1942 and
down to independence. In Bihar, the police were infiltrated by former INA
personnel. They went on strike, and almost disintegrated. Numbers, too,
varied unaccountably. In Bengal, with a population of 60 million, there
were 37,000 police. The UP with 53 million had 49,000 police.

1 May 1948. Some had hoped that these joint agencies might be the means of salvaging something, however meagre, of the former unity of India. But where there was no will for co-operation there could be no way.

Of the two works on the transfer of power by British authors which have received most attention, Leonard Mosley's *The Last Days of the British Raj* places the blame for the dreadful massacres which disfigured independence upon the British policy-makers; most of all upon Mountbatten. He even asserts that partition was unnecessary (p. 247): 'A little patience and all the troubles might have been avoided. Pakistan was the one-man achievement of Mohammad Ali Jinnah, and Jinnah was dead within a year of Pakistan's foundation.' Michael Edwardes, in *The Last Years of British India*, although critical of aspects of British policy, accepts that there was a need for accelerating the transfer of power and says of the Punjab killings (p. 223): 'This particular suffering and bitterness could not be placed at the door of the British, for they were free at last from the responsibilities of ruling an alien people.' V. P. Menon, the man who saw it all through, is content to point out (p. 434) that 'It is easy to be wise after the event'.

Pakistan, and the alternatives

Without attempting to postulate an ideal solution, how far can one assess the capacity of the alternative proposals made during 1946 and 1947 from the British side to provide for a peaceable transfer of power, and a lasting settlement to follow? The Cabinet Mission Scheme would have created something like the Dual Monarchy of Austria–Hungary, if the British concept of the Scheme had been accepted. Under the Dual Monarchy, Hungary was very much the junior partner; and clearly the Group

A would have tended to dominate Groups B and C. However, in the India of today, West Bengal and Punjab have come out at the top in terms of economic development. The advance made in industrialization in Pakistan's Punjab, and more recently in East Bengal, has also been in sharp contrast to the stagnation found in some areas of the sub-continent today. It seems highly probable that undivided and independent Punjab and Bengal would have attained an even more impressive rate of economic growth. Much would have depended on the manner in which foreign aid was channelled: whether to the centre or to the groups (and this would have been a fertile field for disagreement), but if one assumes that the B and C groups had access to credit from abroad, it appears probable that they would have emerged as the most dynamic areas of the sub-continent, well able to take care of their own interests. It is also arguable that the groups would have promoted a healthy regionalism. Bengal and Assam would have soon developed a regional political personality to replace the morbid religious schizophrenia which was so dominant immediately before partition. Even in the north-west it is probable that in Group B the Muslims and Sikhs would have established a *modus vivendi* after (no doubt) tough and sometimes tense bargaining; and this would have been to their mutual advantage.[7] If the north-west and east had been seen to flourish, it is most probable that within a few years there would have been a demand for regional autonomy from other areas: certainly, from the south, and probably from the west coast. A genuinely regional India could have

---

[7] In 1958 I toured among villages in Sheikhupura District in West Pakistan. Talking to some peasants about their crops, they said, 'You know, when the Sikhs lived here they were always planting new crops, or trying new kinds of seed. We had to keep our end up then. We had to make the best use of the canal water, and argue for our full share. We had to be lively (*chalak*). It isn't the same, now the Sikhs have gone.'

avoided the extremes of rigid centralization and the local-
ism of the linguistic states. Genuine regionalism might
have provided the means for the sub-continent to emerge
from the obsession with religious divisions which has
marred every effort to bring together India and Pakistan
and which reached its nadir in the war of September 1965.

The Cabinet Mission Scheme demanded a readiness to
accept a political system in which 'live and let live' would
have been the guiding spirit. Nothing was less in evidence
in 1946, and one is therefore driven to speculate how the
plan which Wavell devised as an alternative would have
worked out. Because the Wavell plan never went any
further than a preliminary draft, and was never discussed
in public, it is not comparable with the Scheme and the
Deal. But it does (and did) deserve serious consideration.
It was hardly an adequate criticism to dismiss it as conceding Pakistan, when twelve months later Pakistan was
conceded all round. Its main attraction was that it did
keep the options open a little longer. The Congress could
have grasped the realities of power, for which so many of
its leaders were hungry, and taken into their hands the
administration of three-quarters of the sub-continent.[8]
Faced with a political situation in the north-west and east
in which the Muslims were demonstrably the strongest
party, they could then have decided whether to negotiate
a deal with the League, whether to leave the Pakistan
areas to go their own way, or whether to put the issue to
the test of force. The latter alternative was unlikely to have
been adopted, in the light of the experiences of Congress
from August 1942 onward, and the choice would have

[8] This judgement on the power-hunger of Congress is not mine but
Gandhi's. In conversation with Dr Zakir Hussain, later Vice-President of
India, in December 1947, Gandhi declared 'Today, everybody in the
Congress is running after power'. Later he said 'the taste for political power
has turned their heads' (see D. G. Tendulkar, *Mahatma: Life of Mohandas
Karamchand Gandhi* (Delhi, rev. ed. 1960–3), viii. 229, 248).

been between some version of the Dual Monarchy model
or partition. If partition had been decided, then the
British administration and British army would have been
concentrated already in the areas where the communities
were most evenly balanced, and a properly controlled
scheme of partition could have been carried through. The
Sikhs would have had some short experience of living in an
embryo Pakistan, and they might have seen their way
clear to making a firm bargain. The great disadvantage
of this plan would have been that a communal war of succession might have broken out in the north-west, while the
British were still formally responsible, which they might
have been unable to suppress. The last months of the
British mandate in Palestine provide a warning of what
might have been, on a wider scale, in Punjab.

Agreement through attrition

The final Mountbatten Deal had the great advantage of
being accepted by Congress and the League. By a long
process of attrition, the two major parties had reached the
stage when they were prepared to acquiesce in a solution
which neither would have considered twelve months
earlier. Could Mountbatten have done any more to bring
home to the peoples of India that (however unwelcome
partition might be to some) this was their decision, freely
made, without pressure from the British? A referendum
was held in the Frontier Province and in Sylhet: could a
referendum have been carried out right across the sub-
continent, so that all could participate in this epochal
decision? If this was too much, would it have been feasible
to organize a referendum in Punjab and Bengal? If there
had been a simple question—'Do you want to belong to
India (Hindustan) or Pakistan?'—and if the voting had
been carefully tabulated, district by district and village by
village, the persons responsible for demarcating the divid-

ing line would have had solid evidence of the will of the people on which to proceed. Those who knew, said that it was impossible to carry out such a referendum successfully. It might have had some unpredictable results: suppose that the partial boycott which occurred in the NWFP had been followed by all, or a sizeable proportion of non-Muslims in Bengal or Punjab? What machinery could have been devised to satisfy the politicians that there was no bias among the officials responsible? Would such a referendum have had a calming effect, or would there have been hysterical propaganda campaigns, terrorization, and corruption on a massive scale?

With all these hazards, the possibility of a reference to the people remains the main aspect of the Deal which may be questioned. The accelerated time-scale, as we have seen, also provides ample scope for argument: but one hesitates to find fault with one of the few British leaders in the post-war period to take time by the forelock. Too often, British political leaders have assumed that 'time is on our side', and always they have been proved wrong. Did Mountbatten's action set a precedent for the accelerated decolonization which marked the end of British rule in Africa, with such dubious consequences? One other acceleration in independence-making may have derived from the Indian example and was certainly proved right: the decision to bring forward independence in Malaya, in the last stage, by more than twelve months.[9] Elsewhere, acceleration had to be answered for: after the transfer of power.

The agreement to disagree

One feature of Mountbatten's Deal must be applauded. He acknowledged the cleft between the communities, and

[9] Both sides—the Malayan national leaders, and the British colonial authority—studied the Indian example closely and borrowed techniques freely from the Indian model.

insisted that the leaders must agree to disagree before British authority was withdrawn. In subsequent constitutional settlements British governments tended to paper over the differences, leaving their successors to sort them out, whether peaceably, as between Malaysia and Singapore, or bloodily, as in Nigeria and Uganda. Mountbatten did not evade this issue: nor, to do them justice, did Wavell and the Cabinet Mission. It was a tragedy that India had to be divided: it would have been a worse tragedy if the issue between Congress, the League and the Sikhs had been submerged in a general *mêlée*.

Strategy and tactics

The question whether the transfer could have been better handled will always remain open to argument. The approach adopted by the main participants in the long debate during 1946 and 1947 provides us with some clues as to why things went as they did. Among the participants, some thought mainly in terms of strategy; some in terms of tactics. On the British side, Wavell and Cripps can both be identified as strategists, Mountbatten and Attlee as tacticians. Wavell's initial strategy was based upon the belief that Pakistan was not a viable solution to the problem. Therefore it was necessary to take a decision on the Pakistan issue: and then, when this was disposed of, some form of united India would inevitably have to be accepted. To Wavell it seemed that Congress strategy was a form of attrition, to which the only reply was to wear out the Congress. As Wellington said at Waterloo, 'Hard pounding, gentlemen; let us see who can pound the longest'. This dual policy was the foundation of all Wavell's actions until the autumn of 1946, when he deduced from the communal riots in Calcutta, Bengal, and Bihar that the British could no longer control the battle:

thereafter he saw no solution but early withdrawal. Cripps also thought in terms of laying down general principles or policies. First, he conceived that the way to break the deadlock was actually to confront the opposing parties with a plan (clearly he had absorbed Toynbee's idea of 'challenge and response'). Later, he hoped that the necessary sense of urgency might be aroused in the Indian leaders by confronting them with a deadline. All Cripps's sympathies were, of course, given to Nehru and the Congress Socialists; yet when the Congress attempted to manipulate the Cabinet Mission Scheme in such a way as to eliminate its essential feature—grouping—in order to take all power, the high sense of principle by which Cripps conducted his life counted for more than his sympathies. He could not go back upon his commitment to a deadline for independence; and so the logic of the situation led Cripps to accept partition as the only solution.

Tactical mastery

Attlee, by contrast, appears as a pure tactician in the context of his dealings with India. Of course, he had a clear long-term policy—to give India independence. But apart from a desire to see the sub-continent remain in the Commonwealth (and this was expendable, as the Burma decision indicated), he had no fixed ideas on what should be done or how it should be done. His colleagues appear to have shared the sense of gathering doom which began to overtake Wavell. Attlee seems to have adopted an almost Micawberish attitude to the problem: something was bound to turn up. Years later, he declared his opinion of the Indian political leaders: 'They would talk and talk and talk'.[10] Did Attlee perceive that Nehru's warnings of a coming struggle against the British were only talk, and

[10] Williams, p. 208.

that hasty emergency actions were not necessary? Attlee's choice of Mountbatten as Viceroy was his greatest tactical move: and his readiness to follow the successive sallies in search of agreement, which the Viceroy mounted, required a combination of steadiness and flexibility. It was Mountbatten's capacity for tactical manoeuvre that brought off the final coup. Proceeding to India with instructions to obtain a settlement embracing Indian unity, he rapidly decided that only partition would work. Beginning from the premise that the Indian army must be maintained intact, he decided to divide the army. At Simla he countered Nehru's bid to disengage from the commitment to partition by a move of such dexterity that most writers have concluded that Mountbatten scrapped his plan in favour of one evolved by V. P. Menon, whereas in reality he preserved his Deal virtually intact. It seems, in assessing the relative importance of strategy and tactics, that the latter carried the day.

But in the submission of the present writer, Mountbatten's achievement was made possible by the groundwork of Wavell. Because Wavell was so clearly labouring to obtain a settlement based upon fundamental principles, he succeeded at last in convincing the Indian leaders that Britain meant to follow words by deeds. He did not succeed in his appeal to the Congress to enter into a new relationship of trust; but he did not altogether fail. After the announcement of his departure on 20 February 1947, Abul Kalam Azad expressed his appreciation:

We cannot doubt his sincerity or integrity of purpose. Nor can I forget that the credit for the changed atmosphere in Indo-British relations today must be traced back to the steps which he so courageously took in June 1945.

It was Wavell's fate to devote eighteen months to a fruitless effort to bring the opposed leaders together. He did not succeed: but he did demonstrate that neither party could force its solution upon the other. When Mount-batten arrived, he only had to open an unlocked door. The two opponents realized that partition was the only solu-tion. But, other Viceroys might not have sensed so quickly that the door was unlocked.

Strategic failings

Can one apply the tactician–strategist distinction to the Indian political leaders? Gandhi was a strategist who at times tried to act like a tactician. He was not suited to that part, and it damaged his capacity to exercise his true strategy. Patel was a real tactician. Among the Congress leaders he was almost certainly the first to grasp that rigidity was not going to gain independence. He saw that if force could not be employed against the British, and if understanding with the League was beyond recall, all that was left was a bargain, a deal. He set himself to bring off the best bargain obtainable.

It is difficult to classify Nehru. He was a strategist, in the sense that he had a clear concept of a united India, and he had a clear view of the way thither: had he not said to Gandhi many years before 'For myself, I delight in war-fare'? Yet, when the crunch came, he was not prepared to stand by either proposition. As a tactician, he lacked that feeling for mood, timing, political temperature, which is so much the attribute of the successful politician. Hardly one of his manoeuvres came off during the whole time from the Scheme to the Deal, and some boomeranged badly, like his insistence upon the provincial right of choice (to stop grouping), his opposition to provincial right of choice ('Balkanization' at Simla), and his insis-tence upon provincial right of choice (independence for the Frontier). Nehru's time was to come: after indepen-dence he earned his reputation, by his work toward building a unified, secular state in the new India. His lapses during 1945–7 went a considerable way towards costing India the unity which might have been preserved.[11]

When considering Jinnah, he emerges as perhaps the greatest tactician of all, British, Hindu, or Muslim. He enjoyed the advantage of always being his own spokesman. Britain spoke through the voices of Wavell, Pethick-Lawrence, Cripps, Attlee, Mountbatten. The Congress was represented successively by Gandhi, Azad, Nehru, and Patel. It was Jinnah first and last.

Pakistan: hope fulfilled and disappointed

Like almost everyone in this story, Jinnah knew what he wanted to see in the future: he wanted Muslim strong-holds, Cities of Refuge, where the Muslim community could plan their own destiny. Jinnah was not a fanatic. If he could be assured that Muslims could get what they wanted within the framework of a Dual Monarchy, a 'Two-Nations' Polity, he appeared ready to temporize. He preferred to continue along the constitutional path where he was so much at home. But he was not prepared to enter any open-ended constitutional scheme, and he was not going to allow what George Orwell once called 'silly-clever' politicians to score at the expense of his party. At the right moment (tactically, not morally) he switched from negotiation to defiance. Then, at the right moment, he chose to take a clipped Pakistan: but one in which the Muslims would be quite unfettered. Among the three pro-tagonists, the British, the Congress, and the League, it was only the latter who reached their desired goal. In some respects Jinnah achieved too much for the Muslims. From

[11] This picture of Nehru is a long way from the hero-worshipping portrait by Michael Brecher which has been generally accepted (*Jawaharlal Nehru, a Political Biography*, 1959). A full-length reassessment of Nehru is overdue; it is not attempted in this essay.

having been a minority—and a somewhat backward minority—they came to be regarded during the vital years 1945–7 as an equal party with the Congress, the equal of the Hindus. The new Pakistan was heralded as the equal of the new India in the Commonwealth (modest little Ceylon never claimed the same status). The Muslims of the north, with their tradition of having been the rulers of India down the centuries, accepted all this as their right. But in truth Pakistan numbered only a quarter of the population of India, which had even greater industrial power *pro rata*. When the day of reckoning came at last, in the aftermath of the September war, Pakistanis had to face the agonizing reality that they did not have the strength of India, a country four times larger. It might have been better if this realization had been forced on them earlier.

However, it must also be said that though Jinnah brilliantly realized the aspirations of the Muslims, his was not a one-man performance, as Mr Mosley and others have suggested.[12] The triumph of the 1945–6 elections was the foundation on which Jinnah's confrontation with Congress and the British was staged. One man may, personally, lose a general election; but one man alone cannot win a general election. The Muslim vote was delivered to the League by the exertions of thousands of 'able missionary lieutenants', as one writer calls them. The same writer, Khalid Bin Sayeed, even goes as far as to suggest that Jinnah was carried farther than he expected to go on the floodtide of Islamic fervour.[13] This was the phenomenon which the Congress leaders never understood, and never accepted—until it was too late.

Altogether, 1947 represented the high tide of the Muslims of India. Having won their Pakistan, they did not know

---

[12] For example, M. Brecher (see *Jawaharlal Nehru*, p. 353).
[13] *Pakistan, the Formative Phase* (Karachi, 1960), pp. 8–9.

what to do with it. All would have been well, perhaps, if partition had put all Muslims into Pakistan and all Hindus into India. But partition only exacerbated the communal problem. Moreover, the anglicized lawyers who provided the new governing class could not, and did not wish to, behave like *mujahids*, fighters for Islam. What ought Pakistan to be, as a political force? The leaders of the country have spent twenty years in trying to answer this question, and have experienced much tribulation on the way.

Emergent India

The Congress, which has been exhibited in these pages in a somewhat equivocal role, went on to prove its true worth in the years after independence. Having resolved its own internal doubts about its commitment to constitutionalism it proceeded to add a new dimension to parliamentary government. It was demonstrated that a democratic system can succeed in a society where a high proportion of the people are (in the formal sense) illiterate and where the women are only just emerging from segregation. And yet, with all its virtues, the governing Congress party continues to maintain that it has a monopoly right to represent the people as the only genuine 'Freedom Movement'. There is much talk of consensus as a virtue by political leaders: but consensus always turns out to mean that all should come under the Congress umbrella.

Departed Britain

What of the British, the other side of the triangle? It soon became clear that Winston Churchill's alarums about the eclipse of the British Empire, and A. V. Alexander's sturdy reminders of Britain's responsibilities to the minority peoples under her care, awakened no response at all from politicians or people. August 1947 demonstrated that British governments of whatever political complexion could dispose of the remaining imperial possessions as soon as they wished. The politicians were not slow to dismantle 'the imperial museum'.[14] There were no agonizing inquests and indictments, as in France after the loss of Vietnam and Algeria. There were no attempts to perpetuate the glories of the British Empire in India, either in stone or in writing: a memorial tablet in Westminster Abbey; at Sandhurst, a hideously ugly monument to the old Indian army in the chapel, and a museum displaying the splendid uniforms of Bengal Lancers; at Oxford, the university commemorated the long and honourable connexion of her sons with the ICS by pulling down the Indian Institute, in order to put up an office for clerks. It remains to be seen whether the Institutes of South Asian Studies at Cambridge and in the School of Oriental and African Studies in London can do something to keep alive the study of India and Pakistan. For one of the saddest aspects of the British withdrawal was the way in which those whose lives had been spent in the Indian service echoed Kipling:

> But that's all shoved behind us,
> Long ago and far away.

Francis Tuker, Lord Birdwood, Ian Stephens, Philip Mason, Penderel Moon, Olaf Caroe; a few still kept up the old tradition of the soldiers and administrators who were scholars. But most chose to put it all aside.

---

[14] The phrase occurs in D. K. Fieldhouse, *The Colonial Empires* (1966) and is not meant to apply to the Commonwealth Institute in South Kensington, though that has its own little *apercus* into the relations between Britain and South Asia today. In the map in the Indian exhibit, Kashmir is shown as a part of India. In the map in the Pakistan exhibit, Kashmir is shown as a part of Pakistan.

In the British army a dwindling remnant of old soldiers still tell their comrades to put a *jaldi* in it, have a *dekko* or *chuprao*, while Gurkha battalions transferred to the British army have gone on to write more pages of faithful service in Malaya, Sabah, and Sarawak.

The forgotten freedom

So far as the British public is concerned, India and Pakistan have been forgotten. After the Indo-Pakistan war, allegations were made in India that Britain was over-partial to Pakistan, and the old myth that Britain had created Pakistan in order to perpetuate the technique of Divide and Rule was dragged out again. All this caused not a ripple in Britain. This indifference is extended to the Indians and Pakistanis living in our midst. They are an 'invisible' community. Their identity is lumped by most British people in with that of West Indians as 'the coloureds'. So, for the British, the great experiment in freedom has ended—not with a bang, not with a whimper or a small cheer—but just in apathy. It is the purpose of this essay to attempt to make some slight impression on that apathy.

Other essays in this series

BALLOT BOX AND BAYONET
People and Government in Emergent
Asian Countries
HUGH TINKER

THE POLITICS OF THE THIRD WORLD
J. D. B. MILLER

THE CHINA-INDIA BORDER
The Origins of the Disputed Boundaries
ALASTAIR LAMB

OXFORD UNIVERSITY PRESS